Charles Dickens

The Greatest Novelist of the Victorian Era

(The True Story of the Life & Time of the Great Author)

Charles Roberge

Published By **Ryan Princeton**

Charles Roberge

All Rights Reserved

Charles Dickens: The Greatest Novelist of the Victorian Era (The True Story of the Life & Time of the Great Author)

ISBN 978-1-7753142-7-1

No part of this guidebook shall be reproduced in any form without permission in writing from the publisher except in the case of brief quotations embodied in critical articles or reviews.

Legal & Disclaimer

The information contained in this book is not designed to replace or take the place of any form of medicine or professional medical advice. The information in this book has been provided for educational & entertainment purposes only.

The information contained in this book has been compiled from sources deemed reliable, and it is accurate to the best of the Author's knowledge; however, the Author cannot guarantee its accuracy and validity and cannot be held liable for any errors or omissions. Changes are periodically made to this book. You must consult your doctor or get professional medical advice before using any of the suggested remedies, techniques, or information in this book.

Upon using the information contained in this book, you agree to hold harmless the Author from and against any damages, costs, and expenses, including any legal fees potentially resulting from the application of any of the information provided by this guide. This disclaimer applies to any damages or injury caused by the use and application, whether directly or indirectly, of any advice or information presented, whether for breach of contract, tort, negligence, personal injury, criminal intent, or under any other cause of action.

You agree to accept all risks of using the information presented inside this book. You need to consult a professional medical practitioner in order to ensure you are both able and healthy enough to participate in this program.

Table Of Contents

Chapter 1: Where Life Began 1

Chapter 2: Charles And Maria 11

Chapter 3: Love, Lust, Infidelity.............. 33

Chapter 4: Dickens In America 59

Chapter 5: Close Brush With Death........ 70

Chapter 6: Mesmerism 89

Chapter 7: The Start Of His Life.............. 98

Chapter 8: His Earliest Novels 108

Chapter 9: The Years Inside The Middle 117

Chapter 10: The Late Years 123

Chapter 11: "Our Mutual Friend" With The Resource Of Charles Dickens................ 127

Chapter 12: A Christmas Carol With The Aid Of The Use Of The Usage Of Charles Dickens 141

Chapter 13: The Marriage Of Charles Dickens 157

Chapter 14: The Kids Of Charles Dickens
.... 163

Chapter 15: Master Of His Own Future 169

Chapter 16: Dark Days For Charles Dickens
.... 179

Chapter 1: Where Life Began

No one is vain on this global who lightens the weight of it to all of us else.

Charles Dickens

Some people dwelling within the twenty first century, except those who have studied "literature" in university in the twentieth and twenty first century, not often understand about this man besides his ebook and movie 'A Christmas Carol' that offers actual that means to what Christmas is all approximately and for what Dickens is maximum stated and remembered.

He modified into moreover a pretty influential and prolific British writer of the nineteenth century who had written such remarkable works like 'Oliver Twist,' 'David Copperfield' and one known as 'Great Expectations.'

To understand Charles Dickens aka Charles John Huffman Dickens, it's far crucial to recognize about his life from starting to the give up. Charles Dickens changed into born in England, Portsmouth, (at that point it turn out to be known as Portsea) Hampshire at the southern coastal a part of England on February 7th, 1812. He have become born to John and Elizabeth Dickens. Elizabeth Dickens, Charles Dickens' mother, whose maiden name modified into Elizabeth Barrow, aspired to be a teacher or university director. John Dickens, a naval clerk, had constantly dreamed of setting it rich.

It so passed off that Charles turned into the second one toddler of 8 kids. His dad served due to the fact the payroll clerk at the navy workplace. Due to their monetary troubles, the Dickens circle of relatives needed to waft about until they in the end settled in Camden Town which emerge as in a lousy segment of London.

It emerge as a unhappy truth that when Charles Dickens modified into twelve years antique, he became already running and he had to expose his again on his children to turn out to be a jogging-elegance boy and act like a person in the manufacturing unit to make black.

It modified into crucial that Charles had to stroll five miles to art work, paintings for ten hours after which walk 5 miles again to his rented room. He first-class observed his family on Sunday at the same time as he could cross go to his Dad at the London Marshalsea jail to visit him.

The rest of the family except one of Charles sisters resided within the jail.

The period of shame to Charles regarded to overshadow his entire existence and via some way colored all his writing.

Dickens, in his fictional writing, wrote about the overlooked, abused and parentless children even these days after one hundred and fifty years remains felt thru the use of every reader.

At this run-down, but rodent infested manufacturing facility, Charles changed into earning six shillings every week for placing labels on pots of the "blacking," cloth getting used for cleansing fireplaces. It become all he want to do at twelve years vintage to help in supporting his own family.

When Dickens might appearance once more at this a part of his existence and the memories that got here with it, he appeared to sense that it changed into the moment that he stated goodbye to all his kids, and felt he had been forged away by using way of manner of his dad and mom at this form of younger age. It made him revel in betrayed and abandoned with the aid of all of the adults which have been speculated to be looking after him as a toddler. It seemed that this would be a commonplace thread in his writing in some time.

Charles father needed to serve time in debtor's jail, and the relaxation of the entire own family moved in order that they'll be close to the jail, and left Charles there via himself to work in the blacking manufacturing unit.

Living via this trouble through the usage of himself changed into in all likelihood one of the most large additives of his existence. It tainted his view on existence and the sector as an entire, and he might later use it and describe it nicely in plenty of his novels.

When Charles Dickens have become very extra youthful, even then he desired to turn out to be a gentleman. He dreamed of getting an education. It modified right into a strong preference he couldn't give up on.

Charles Dickens dad and mom had a few limited charge variety they had positioned lower lower back to try to deliver at the least one in all their youngsters to college or maybe an academy. Mom and Dad Dickens felt that the qualifications and competencies of all their children put together and decided that they should use their money which have been earmarked for schooling in the place in which it'd benefit the maximum. It appeared to in truth every body like they were setting all their chips on one infant; similar to on the online on line casino. However, Charles changed into now not to be that infant. Instead, Charles dad and mom decided to supply his sister, Fanny, to college. She seemed to be very proficient in song and became then sent off to the academy.

After Charles father acquired an inheritance and will pay off his money owed, Charles modified into then capable of go back to school!

When Charles have become fifteen in 1827, he changed into pressured to depart school and go again to art work, this time he is probably walking as an workplace boy. The next three hundred and sixty five days

Charles Dickens have end up a stenographer (he became using shorthand and transcribing his files) and a settlement reporter for the courts of regulation in London.

In 1827 he additionally enrolled at Wellington House Academy as a scholar and turn out to be capable of gain a feature with Ellis and Blackmore Law Firm.

As a law clerk, he have become required to preserve up with the petty cash fund, deliver documents of the court, strolling errands for the courtroom and different duties as wished.

November 1828, Charles Dickens moved to a one of a kind however comparable feature with the Charles Molley Law Firm. Dickens simplest stayed some quick months with this corporation.

But for Dicken's, the law changed into not appealing to him for a career. He became starting to get bored with being a law clerk, and it turned into feeling tedious to him. When he concept approximately it, to come to be a criminal professional wasn't appealing to him anymore each. He decided it became time to look for a few other manner of creating a residing.

Dicken's located his next way as a court docket docket stenographer. So he may additionally need to qualify for that unique position, Dickens needed to gain knowledge of within the Gurney shorthand gadget. For the bulk of humans learning this gadget, it took 3 years to look at the entire device and strategies. Dickens, but, had an super reminiscence to paintings with and emerge as able to observe it in 3 months. It is cited that Charles Dickens I.Q. The score have become a hundred and eighty. It emerge as in 1829 he started operating as a contract courtroom docket stenographer.

Then in 1831 Dickens commenced out as a shorthand strolling with the "Mirror of Parliament." The file end up for giving bills of what have become taking vicinity within the House of Lords and the House of Commons. Charles Dickens soon changed into diagnosed all through England for his accurate and activate reporting inside the court docket docket as well.

Dickens stated he had ultimately tamed the mystery of stenography and may make a reasonably decent residing with the abilities. It appears he was highly genuine for the accomplishments he had received together along with his shorthand artwork and he knew 11 others within the place that could assist with reporting any debates that got here up in Parliament for the Morning Newspaper.

Dickens said that he should circulate night time after night time recording predictions that could in no manner see the moderate of day with motives that handiest mystified others.

Dickens stated he felt as though he wallowed in terms. During this era Dickens notion approximately pursuing an appearing profession. He become severe while it came to performing, so he even made an appointment for an audition with the Lyceum Theater. Unfortunately, he became sick at the day of his audition and changed into now not capable of head. He had acting competencies which were proven through his performances and readings in his advantage productions. You in no way apprehend what path his lifestyles might also have taken if he had no longer been sick the day of his audition.

It is maximum interesting that later in his profession that Dickens worked acting into his writing profession. During 1858 he started out giving professional readings, and from then on he endured to attain this in some unspecified time within the destiny of his life. He made the readings a aggregate of passionate and oratory performing.

Chapter 2: Charles And Maria

The pain of parting isn't always something to the delight of meeting once more.

Charles Dickens

Charles grow to be dissatisfied with how his profession modified into progressing, and he modified into on foot to make a higher affect with Maria's own family which lead him to do not forget becoming an actor. Charles went to date to be granted an audition. It passed off that Charles got here down ill the day of his audition and wound up lacking his appointment. Charles cherished, the more youthful Maria, added on him to be later inspired for the man or woman in David Copperfield for the girl function of Dora.

It will in no way be regarded of the 'actual' affections that Maria felt approximately Charles. Sometimes, Maria may deal with him in a manner to encourage him to reveal affection for her and other instances may additionally deal with him with stylish indifference. Maria did declare in a while in lifestyles that she had cared for Charles, but who is aware of if she spoke the truth at that point?

When Charles grew to emerge as twenty-one within the early part of 1833, he gave himself a "coming-of-age" blow-out birthday celebration. He invited the Beadnell's, and they popular the invitation lots to his surprise. Charles Dickens in the end in the midnight discovered Maria and have been given her to himself. He suggested her of his feelings for her. She have become on him with insults with the aid of way of calling him a "boy."

What little relationship that they had, ended that 12 months. Maria went directly to marry Henry Winter. But mother and father, that is not to be the completing of that love story.

They had had no contact for twenty-four years after being separated, Maria made touch and reached out to Charles. At the time, they each had been married and at the identical time as Dickens lacked any prospect at the same time as greater younger, had now come to be a famous writer.

Charles changed into ecstatic whilst he obtained Maria's letter. It delivered floods of memories about how excessive his love had been for her and perhaps some fantasies of what might have been.

So, in 1855 Maria and Charles agreed to meet in thriller without their spouses. Maria forewarned Dickens that she regarded nowhere much like the same younger lady he had as soon as remembered. Even despite the fact that she had warned him, he appeared stunned at how she had modified from what she have grow to be even as he first loved her. She had received an entire lot of weight. (Do guys no longer ever take into account how they have modified as properly?)

Charles and Maria met once more for dinner with their spouses. After that, Maria did now not surrender, and Maria permit him recognize she preferred similarly contact a number of the two, Charles Dickens persisted to avoid her.

By the time 1832 rolled round Charles modified right into a reporter for two one among a kind London newspapers and then inside the next yr, he commenced contributing a chain of his sketches and impressions out to superb magazines and newspapers, and he would probable use a fake name of "Boz." The specific London scenes of London lifestyles reached an extended manner in organising Dickens' reputation, and that they've been posted at some point of 1836 in his first ebook.

CHARLES AND HIS CHILDREN

In the little global wherein children have their existence, whosoever brings them up, there can be not anything so finely perceived and so finely felt, as injustice.

Charles Dickens

The Children of Charles and Catherine Dickens gave the arena ten Dickens youngsters.

There has been 'circumstantial' evidence exceptional that Ellen Ternan and Charles Dickens had a infant together, however it expired swiftly after begin. The fact has in no manner been tested.

CHARLES CULLIFORD BOZ DICKENS (BIRTH 1837 – DEATH 1896)

Charles modified into said via the usage of the own family as Charley, and come to be the oldest of all of Charles Dickens children.

Charley started running in the commercial enterprise business enterprise and banking existence. In 1868 he needed to claim monetary smash, after which his father hired him on as an employee to paintings there at "All The Year Round." It have become later while Charley commenced writing reference books. "Dickens' Dictionary of the Thames" and "Dickens' Dictionary of London." Charley sold "Gad's Hill Place" after his dad had died, and later gave it all up due to the truth he have turn out to be so ill. He changed into fifty nine while he died in 1896.

MARY DICKENS (BIRTH 1838 – DEATH 1896)

Mary were named after her aunt, her mom's sister that had died in 1837. After her Dad died, Mary lived with Georgina, her aunt. Mary, a creator as nicely, went on to install writing the ebook, "My Father as I Recall Him."

KATE MACREADY DICKENS (BIRTH 1839 – DEATH 1929)

When Catherine and Dickens separated, Kate have become the exceptional one of the children that stood up in competition to her Father and took facets together along with her mom, Catherine. It need to have in no manner amazed Dickens because of the truth Kate have been nicknamed "Lucifer's Box" in the circle of the family because of her fiery temper. Kate married Charles Allston Collins after which after he died she remarried Carlo Perugini.

WALTER LANDOR DICKENS (BIRTH 1841 – DEATH 1863)

Walter had been named after the extremely good poet and creator, Walter Savage Landor.

Walter had completed the rank of lieutenant with the East India Company. It modified into searching as although he had a destiny in advance of him that modified into vibrant, then unluckily, matters started falling apart for Walter. He and maximum of his circle of relatives individuals fell onto difficult instances with debt. It became about this equal time that Walter began out getting sick. He died of an aortic aneurysm, and it delivered about him to go away masses of unpaid money owed to his Dad.

FRANCIS JEFFREY DICKENS (BIRTH 1844 – DEATH 1886)

Francis had been given the nickname of "Chickenstalker" via his Dad. His character call from then on end up "The Chimes."

Francis Jeffrey being five of ten of the kids and being from the parents of Charles and wife Catherine. Francis changed into born in England, in London on January 15, 1844. The twelve months earlier than on Christmas had visible what a first-rate fulfillment the "Christmas Carol" had turn out to be.

Francis idea approximately hundreds of careers that included farming, journalism, and treatment. He decided in the end to sign up in the Mounted Police of Bengal. Later on, he have grow to be part of Canada's Northwest Mounted Police. It changed into in 1886 while he resigned his charge, and internal a 365 days, he have become long long gone for all time.

The English who had coins had a life-style of sending their children off to boarding college. When he have emerge as an early age, Francis Jeffrey changed into despatched off to attend a boarding college for English boys' in Boulogne, France.

In only some years Francis Jeffrey had started out out writing from a college in Hamburg, Germany. Here wherein he become decided unsuccessful at the equal time as reading his pre-clinical subjects. When he yet again to London, he joined employment for a quick at the equal time as alongside along together with his Dad's mag. It have been said that inside the beyond that Francis had been a piece difficult listening to and will stutter once in a while.

Francis went to India in 1863 to serve along the Bengal Lancers. When his father died in 1870, Francis Jeffrey went decrease back to England. After four years he acquired a commission to be a Sub-Inspector in what modified into known as the contemporary usual Mounted Police in the North West and sailed off to Canada. He had been given there too past due to be worried in what they might ultimately name 'The North West of the NWMP' within the summer season of 1874. He modified into then sent to the placed up of Fort Dufferin that lay near the forty ninth parallel at some point of the wintry weather of 1874-1875.

Then, in 1875 he modified into sent to be stationed at the Swan River at Fort Livingston and immediately to Fort Macleod. Both of the postings known as for prolonged hours the usage of inside the saddle journeying on the pony for what regarded like countless hours on the prairie. The next 12 months all the American Great

Plains and Canadian Plains determined themselves to be in turmoil after Custer's massacre and all of his men on the 'Battle of Little Big Horn' with the aid of the usage of the Chief Sitting Bull and all of his warriors. We find out that each of the countries had been staying on conflict alert due to the truth the aborigines outnumbered the whites.

After Sitting Bull massacred the Sixth Cavalry and Custer in 1876 with tensions in the course of the complete place have been excessive. Fort Pitt had grow to be the coronary heart of one of the most explosive regions in which you could find out Big Bear of the Metis and the Crees have been all in a country of unrest. There seemed to be ongoing troubles about Louis Riel that had started out the Red River Rebellion inside the path of 1870 might then move decrease returned from a few self-imposed exile up in Montana to influence in greater uprisings.

The subsequent three hundred and sixty five days in 1877 Cypress Hills determined that Sitting Bull had moved there; but, he have turn out to be below the cautious however watchful eyes at Wood Mountain and Fort Walsh through way of the NWMP. Sitting Bull and all his tribe would possibly stay within the Canadian territory for about three years. In 1877 on the equal time as Dickens became stationed at Fort Macleod, he changed into present there on the Blackfoot Crossing at the time of the signing for Treaty Number Seven together with the Blackfoot Indians.

In 1878 Dickens, Sub Inspector were given transferred to Fort Walsh wherein he appeared to overlap with the famous Sitting Bull. 1879 located Francis Jeffrey though stationed at For Walsh and it became this yr his mother did die after which turn out to be buried in Highgate Cemetery, London. (His well-known father, the writer, became buried in Westminster Abbey). In November

1879 Constable Grayburn of the NWMP have grow to be murdered at the same time as attending the horses at the same time as near Fort Walsh, and it led him to the prolonged tensions in that location.

In 1880 inside the direction of June, Dickens received a advertising up to the rank of Inspector after which transferred to Fort Macleod from Fort Walsh. The subsequent one year "Chickenstalker" moved to 'Blackfoot Crossing' down at the Bow River that have become approximately 50 miles east of Fort Calgary. He have turn out to be involved with on the minimal one confrontation with a courageous (Indian) that had stolen himself a horse. The incident changed into in the end settled through the clever intervention through using Chief Crowfoot and with the help of the employees of the NWMP that forced the march from Fort Macleod.

Dickens stayed there at Blackfoot Crossing for all of 1881 and the number one six months of 1882 and modified into fine there will be huge changes in the usa with all the westward advancement of production for the Canadian Pacific Railway.

It won't be important for the dusty, laborious path marches being made to visit Fort Benton, Montana Territory that sat at the Missouri River and then catch what become referred to as a paddle wheeler that changed into headed for Bismark in North Dakota to lure rail transportation going east. While Dickens served his 12 years serving with NWMP, he need to never go away the frontier.

Then in 1883, Dickens observed himself being transferred to Fort Pitt that lay on the North Saskatchewan River and turned into located in price of a poorly however small positioned castle that lay along the what turn out to be taken into consideration the primary river that served as their highway deliver direction among Fort Edmonton and Fort Carlton.

The Inspector Dickens should again and again warn others of the unrest in that area, and while March 1885 rolled around, it all blew up with the NWMP struggling with at Duck Lake. They had been then located with the aid of Fort Carlton being burned then the Crees murdered the priests or even the personnel of the Hudson Bay Company and all the circle of relatives members there at Frog Lake.

The site lay 35 miles north and west of Fort Pitt. Dickens sent 3 of his scouts to appearance what became taking place past them. On their go back, the Cree warriors attacked them; one have been given away unharmed, one wounded and performed useless till it modified into stable so he should then crawl lower once more to the citadel, the alternative by using manner of the decision of Cowan grow to be inside reach of the Fort at the same time as he changed into killed. The Indian warrior reduce out his coronary coronary heart and ate some of it in the front of the defenders which have been already so horrified and dwelling within the castle.

The detachment of the NWMP became outgunned and outnumbered 2 hundred through 20. The Negotiations then caused all of the civilians that would comply with grow to be prisoners of Big Bear and the Cree. The Chief gave Dickens and all his guys a quick length to get out of the fort.

They did and traveled maximum of the ice pans in a leaky scow. Scouts who came from Fort Battleford advised in reality anybody at Fort Pitt were killed, however after six days journeying the river Dickens along with his guys arrived at Battleford and purchased a hero's welcome.

In the Summer of 1885, Inspector Dickens worked due to the fact the Justice of the Peace near Fort Battleford and Fort Pitt wherein he become carrying out some of the preliminary trials of all individuals who have been worried in an revolt near those forts. Come November eighth the ones identical human beings had been found accountable, were hanged to loss of life. It may be later that same month that Regina Louis Riel may additionally meet the same destiny.

Because Dickens had served for twelve years there in the North West, then the assault on Fort Pitt happened, at that factor he became discharged a clinical depart. Before Christmas of that same yr in 1885, he traveled with a scientific orderly journeying overland to visit Swift Current, and from there he went via Canadian Pacific Railway to adventure at once to Regina, Toronto, Winnipeg, Montreal, and Ottawa. He did spend Christmas collectively collectively together with his most cutting-edge friend, Dr. Jamieson who became residing in Ottawa at the time but have become from Moline, Illinois. It might be in March of 1886 at the same time as he in the long run resigned from his military because of his fitness.

Dr. Alexander Jamieson have become an admirer of all of the writings of Francis Jeffrey's Dad, Charles. The 'Chickenstalker' did take shipping of an invite from Dr. Jamieson for him to tour to Moline, Illinois to give a chain of talks approximately what he had professional in the course of the Riel Rebellion inside the 365 days of 1885.

On June 11th he became on the brink of make his scheduled speech and had began out to sit down down all the way down to the dinner in advance than such. He picked up a pitcher of ice water and clutched at his chest as though he were in ache. Those with him took him proper right into a room next door, however he died of what at that point changed into assumed to be a coronary heart assault at the age of 40 two years.

The humans of Moline, Illinois had been so type as to make the arrangements, paid for max all of the funeral and burial fees. After a while there has been a cement marker placed on his grave, after which severa years later a bronze plaque became designed to connect with that particular marker.

ALFRED D'ORSAY TENNYSON DICKENS (BIRTH 1845 – DEATH 1912)

When Alfred have become twenty he left England and all of the many unpaid bills he left in the back of too. From England, he traveled to Australia. In Australia, he wed the "The Belle of Melbourne," Ms. Jessie Devlin. She had left Alfred via way of himself with their girls for 4 years, and she or he or he then died in a carriage damage.

After Charles Dickens, his father died, Alfred began giving lectures approximately his Dad's paintings and life.

SYDNEY SMITH HALDIMAND DICKENS (BIRTH 1847 – DEATH 1872)

One need to admit that Charles Dickens emerge as surprisingly thrilled along with his son Sydney's profession within the Navy. Later in lifestyles, he modified into disillusioned on the same time as Sydney became so harassed with economic problems and Dickens refused to permit him come domestic or to help him financially. In later years, Mamie Dickens, his sister instructed that when she idea approximately her brother Sydney for which the only phrases that might come to her mind were the phrases "horror" or "contempt."

Sydney modified into in provider on the HMS Topaze and feature turn out to be very sick so turn out to be furloughed from the Navy due to his awful fitness in April 1872. They allowed him to passage home on the Topaze to get from India to England wherein he, unluckily, became determined vain some days later at sea. Sydney become buried at sea in the Indian Ocean at the age of twenty-5, and no cause of demise emerge as ever determined.

HENRY FIELDING DICKENS (BIRTH 1849 – DEATH 1933)

The family nicknamed Henry to Harry and he was most customarily call the Dickens' maximum a success infant. He loved being a sportsman and had earned a a achievement regulation career. During 1922 he became knighted.

Henry emerge as a grandpa to Monica Dickens who soon became a well-known writer like her excellent grandpa. One of her works turn out to be "One Pair of Hands."

DORA ANNIE DICKENS (BIRTH 1850 – DEATH 1851)

Dora were named after one of the characters in her Dad's novels, the Dora from his ebook David Copperfield. Dora had in no way been a very healthy infant, and whilst she have end up 8 months vintage, she died.

EDWARD BULWER LYTTON DICKENS (BIRTH 1852 – DEATH 1902)

Edward have been nicknamed Plorn. They named him after the writer Edward Bulwer-Lytton. As an exciting word, there has been the quote "it have turn out to be a darkish and stormy night" that comes from the radical through way of the usage of Paul Clifford.

Edward left England so he should be part of his brother Alfred who modified into in Australia. Later, he have come to be a Member of the Parliament in New South Wales.

Chapter 3: Love, Lust, Infidelity

It is a despair truth that even extraordinary guys have their terrible contributors of the circle of relatives.

Charles Dickens

Because Charles Dickens fulfillment appeared to be strengthening, he determined to marry Catherine Hogarth.

Catherine changed into the oldest daughter of Georgina and George Hogarth, and she or he or he have been born in Scotland. It turned into 1834 while she and her whole own family packed up and moved to England due to the fact her Dad had been hired as the music critic for the Morning Chronicle.

Dickens who emerge as unattached, more youthful and impressionable, emerge as employed at the Morning Chronicle as nicely. Remember if you may that his actual first romance Charles had been concerned in after Maria Beadnell, and that romantic hobby had ended relatively.

He recovered from Maria, and after meeting Catherine, he have become fast taken. They met every different in 1834, were given engaged in the course of 1835 and married in April of 1836.

It have become in 1841 that Catherine and Charles traveled to Scotland as a couple and in 1842 they traveled right now to America together.

After they left the usa, Georgina who became Catherine's sister got here to stay with the new couple. It regarded that Catherine changed into beginning to experience beaten with what modified into required of the spouse of this sort of famous man and being involved for his youngsters at the identical time. Georgina came alongside to fill inside the gaps, and at the same time as you consider that Catherine couldn't manipulate a good buy, Georgina in the end ran the whole Dickens domestic. Georgina even took Charles side even as it came to the divorce, saying that Catherine overlooked her children all of the time.

Charles modified into developing unhappy with Catherine and their marriage. He felt like numerous he did grow to be work all the time so he may also want to resource all of his kids, and it made him hate Catherine even extra. In his thoughts having those many youngsters modified into all Catherine's fault. He hated that Catherine seemed like she had no power, no strain to do some thing. He felt and started out indicating that she became NOT clever or maybe from the beginning had now not however all commenced to be equal to his intellect.

It emerge as in 1857 that Charles Dickens met the woman who might be a partner to him until he died. Her call modified into Ellen Ternan. Ellen, her sister, and her mom had been all employed for a benefit presentation to act in "The Frozen Deep." Dickens' backed the complete occasion, and he co-starred as well.

When Dickens appeared decrease back on his existence with Catherine, he determined out how insufferable it have been after he met Ellen. Dickens had written a letter to his old buddy John Forster wherein he informed him that he and Catherine have been virtually now not intended for every unique and there was simply no fixing it. It was no longer that she most effective made him unhappy or uneasy, however he knew he made her sense the same way too and perhaps even more so.

In 1857 Catherine and Charles give up sound asleep collectively, and each moved into their separate bedrooms.

Dickens left his wife Catherine in 1858 with the resource of separation. He went thus far as to slander her in public and commenced an intimate affair with Ellen "Nelly" Ternan who turn out to be a younger actress.

Sources will let you know specific versions as to whether or no longer the two started out seeing each different earlier than Dickens' broke up along alongside along with his wife or in a while. It is felt that Dickens went to extremes to erase the documentation, so he receives rid of any presence of Ternan in his life.

Charles Dickens digs his grave deeper while he orders his mistress a bracelet, and it gets sent through mistake to his home in which his modern-day-day spouse, Catherine finds it. It almost seems like a singular or a actual romance does it no longer? But, it effective befell to Catherine and Dickens!

It regarded like the earliest a part of their marriage was glad. Charles Dickens grow to be so in love together along with his new more youthful partner, and he or she or he or he appeared to be happy together with her famous new husband.

After Catherine had determined the bracelet, she got here out and accused Charles of getting an affair. Of path, Charles denied the reality that he have become having an affair and brushed it off as it became his manner of letting his actors recognize that he desired their paintings in his plays with the beneficial useful resource of giving them small offers.

A prolonged-out of place letter surfaced in 2012 that installation how Dickens felt closer to his first accomplice within the direction of the end in their marriage. He desired out of the marriage so he need to skip on with the rest of his existence. In the letter, he informed his legal expert to provide Catherine £six hundred every 12 months that's what £25,000 these days.

The letter became located while a proprietor of a residence out within the

Cotswolds at the time they had been performing some spring cleansing and it fell out of a paperback Bible that have been given to them via a neighbor who became being moved out proper proper into a nursing domestic seven or eight years previous.

The letter changed into authenticated and furnished in London thru Fraser's Autographs at an estimate of £1,000 to £1,500.

When the letter end up located it were folded in half of and then tucked within the various Bible's pages adore it had been used as a bookmark.

The flyleaf of this Bible had the call of "James Flanders" with the date of July 0.33, 1870 and the choice "Olive Tempest Flanders," with the date of July 1890. It was inscribed with telling absolutely everyone it were given to the person meant for with the useful resource of using the person's father.

It did now not rely however due to the reality the decision seemed to haven't any connection with the elderly neighbor that had given the e-book away and then died. No you could simply understand why she had the Bible.

The biographer, Michael Slater conveyed to the "Telegraph" right now that he felt the tone of Dickens' letter is just a man so decided to get out of a awful marriage at about any rate and accomplish that as speedy as feasible. Dickens felt it modified into inflicting terrible publicity for him and the marriage became sickening to him.

Charles and Catherine legally separated in June of 1858. It might be a few days later at the same time as Charles may place a word in the "Household Words" and the "London Times" to provide an reason for his or her separation to the general public at big.

He said in his word that he had a few 'home' hassle, which modified into prolonged-reputation, and he might also make no similarly feedback out of understand, because of the private, sacred nature of all of it. It had all been determined on as an affiliation, and there has been no sick-will or any anger. The entire development, starting, and the surrounding instances which have been taking place in a few unspecified time within the destiny of our separation and divorce are inside our kids's understanding. It is all amicable, and the info want to be forgotten so we are capable of go along with the waft on with our lives.

To maximum human beings this will seem intense, putting an statement inside the paper to allow different parents understand which you are retaining apart from your accomplice and what goes on in life might by no means arise on this day and hour.

Yes, there was gossip about some actress or maybe some memories that lay the muse for Dickens to be having an affair without any awesome but Georgina, his live-in sister-in-law. The second rumor turn out to be even worse than even the primary in that a courting like that might were considered incestuous.

It didn't rely variety that Dickens had given assurances to anybody and that they remained pals. The fact end up that Catherine and Dickens were never on pleasant phrases once more. Dickens gave Catherine the house. The oldest boy, Charley decided to live with Catherine and Charles stored custody with the relaxation of their youngsters. He by no means forbade the kids to look her, but he in no manner advocated them every.

It would appear that Catherine lived for twenty more years after she and Charles separated and died in 1879. She, being taken a long way from the location of mom and spouse, but it seemed she in no way did recover over the breakup in their marriage.

FAMOUS WORKS OF DICKENS

It modified into the exquisite of instances, it have become the worst of instances.

Charles Dickens

It have become in 1836 that Charles Dickens commenced out publishing "The Posthumous Papers" for the Pickwick Club each month. It end up in a shape a serial e-book that ultimately have emerge as a widespread way to put in writing and produce fiction for the Victorian duration. Dickens' achievement modified into so excellent with this shape of approach that the "Pickwick" had become one of the maximum well-known and well-known literary works in the path of that factor, and it saved being posted in its e book form in 1837.

It have become after "Pickwick" modified into so a success that Dickens began publishing in reality certainly one of his new novels, "Oliver Twist." He also have become the latest editor of a contemporary-day month-to-month mag called "Bentley's Miscellany." He stored publishing that new novel in all his later magazines, in "Household Worlds" and the one referred to as "All the Year Round." "Oliver Twist" had a manner of expressing Charles Dickens' hobby about existence inside the slums to its very fullest, as an innocent orphans fortunes have been traced thru all London streets preserving all and sundry placing on until the subsequent posted paper.

It is not any doubt that Dickens' career have become a achievement. The next ten years one may additionally need to peer that his books had been no longer engaging within the achievement of his first successes. The works right now had been "Nicholas Nickleby" written within the path of 1838-1839, "The Old Curiosity Shop" within the course of 1840 – 1841, and "Barnaby Rudge" in 1841. Charles Dickens did marry Catherine Hogarth pretty rapid after he wrote the primary ebook, "Sketches with the resource of Boz," were posted.

Dickens decided in 1842 whilst he positioned out that he modified into as famous in the United States as he were in England, that he ought to pass on a talking-lecture tour of the U.S. He can be speakme in competition to slavery and his useful resource of numerous types of reform.

When Dickens lower lower returned to England he started out writing his "American Notes," it have come to be a e-book that criticized American life as being materialistic and culturally backward. He felt it grow to be all characterized through the Americans choice for material items and wealth.

For his subsequent ebook, "Martin Chuzzlewit" (1843 – 1844), it describes in which the hero is locating that staying alive at the brilliant frontier of America is extra difficult than ones way making it to England.

It changed into in the course of the years that Chuzzlewit have emerge as on the scene, that Dickens published special Christmas stories, the only masses extra without issue and speedy remembered with the beneficial useful resource of all, "A Christmas Carol" and "The Chimes."

One is privy to for first-rate in the occasion that they do not maintain in mind some thing else that Charles Dickens is one, if no longer the maximum influential and important writers at a few degree within the 19th century. He had many accomplishments and has been lauded for giving an entire stark portrait of what the Victorian underclass which helped in bringing about some very wished societal alternate.

BOOKS BY CHARLES DICKENS

During Dickens' profession, he did positioned up 15 novels. Some of his wonderful-stated works included:

Soon after Charles Dickens had posted his first ebook, "Sketches through Boz," he married Catherine Hogarth.

It have grow to be a 12 months after being distant places on the equal time as in Italy and at the same time as writing "Pictures from Italy" (1846), that Dickens published "Dombey and Son" installments that continued till 1848. The finished e-book diagnosed there has been a trendy desired with the ultra-modern Dickensian novel and it felt like it became developing a turning thing in his complete career.

As the general call of the ebook specifies, "Dealings with the Firm of Dombey and Son" have become a have a look at on how the have an impact on of values inside the organisation society had with non-public fortunes of households and those with which that family emerge as familiar. It gives a somber view of England inside the path of mid-century, and this tone takes region to emerge as feature of Dickens' future novels.

Charles Dickens' subsequent ebook/novel, "David Copperfield" written in 1849-1850, is what may be taken into consideration the number one recording of a diary of the standard more youthful guy's existence in Victorian England. The autobiographical novel modified proper into a fictionalized version detail that described Dickens' childhood, and his dream and pursuit of his imaginative and prescient for a journalism profession, and a love for lifestyles. Copperfield turn out to be not one among Dickens' most celebrated novels, however it changed into considered his personal favourite.

"Household Words" a modern day mag become commenced out out through Dickens in 1850. His articles and editorials had been touched with social institutions, family life, and English politics. His art work moreover spoke to the fictional kind remedy of the topics found in Dickens' novels. The magazine "Household Words" ran until

1859, after which Dickens commenced out a today's weekly, "All the Year Round." In each the ones guides, he did placed up a number of his most sizable novels.

'Oliver Twist' (1837 – 1838) – have grow to be Dickens' first novel, and it positioned the whole life of an orphan who lived inside the streets. Oliver Twist inspired how Dickens had felt whilst he have come to be an impoverished teen being compelled to barely get by on most effective his wits and seeking to earn his keep in existence. Since Dickens became a Publisher of a mag that grow to be called "Bentley's Miscellany," Dickens started to position up "Oliver Twist" in installments starting in February 1837 to April 1838, and he posted the complete version of the e-book in November 1838.

Dickens saved setting "Oliver Twist" in all the magazines he could probable later edit, that blanketed "All the Year Round" and "Household Words." The novel of "Oliver Twist" was well-obtained in America and

England. The committed those who check "Oliver Twist" with keen anticipation for every subsequent installment that got here out month-to-month.

'A Christmas Carol' (1843)- December nineteenth, 1843 noticed Dickens publishing "A Christmas Carol." The e-book featured the evil but timeless Ebenezer Scrooge, who have come to be an unpleasant antique miser, who, with the help of ghosts beyond, assist him find out his Christmas spirit. Dickens managed to pen the e-book in only some brief six weeks. He started out in October and completed the book right on time for Christmas celebrations. He intended for the unconventional to be a complaint of the social stigma and convey interest to all of the hardships that lots of England's lower elegance had to face every day.

"A Christmas Carol" end up a huge fulfillment and provided over 6,000 copies as quick as it grow to be published. The readers in America and England were all touched due to the ebook's emotional, empathetic intensity, and one American entrepreneur come to be said to have given his personnel one greater day's excursion after he test the ebook.

Regardless of the literary evaluations, the book, "A Christmas Carol" stays to nowadays, considered one among Dickens' most favored and well-known works. It is a timeless piece of work.

When one thinks about it; Charles Dickens and his works probable had even greater have an impact on on how Christians celebrated Christmas than a few different character in information except Jesus Christ himself. When the Victorian age started, celebrating Christmas changed into declining.

The traditions from medieval Christmases combined celebrating Christ's beginning with Roman's pageant celebrating the

Roman god of agriculture, and the German wintry weather Yule competition.

The Industrial Revolution inside the period in-between in records changed into in entire swing all through Dickens lifestyles however allowed the worker's little time to have a laugh Christmas. Charles Dickens contributed plenty to carry decrease again all the traditions of celebrating Christmas.

Then, Prince Albert determined to deliver again the German customs of the manner the Christmas Tree in England come to be adorned, all people making a song Christmas carols (which had pretty a high-quality deal all but disappeared) started out out developing all yet again.

Now, one hundred sixty years later, "A Christmas Carol" nonetheless is relevant and is sending a message that manages to lessen through all the materialism of purchasing presents and spending manner too much money in some unspecified time in the future of the holiday season. Charles Dickens felt that the vacations had been a time for forgiving, being type, to have tremendous instances collectively, so it seemed that it changed into the notable time at a few stage within the 12 months at the same time as others appear to open up their hard hearts and provide freely.

The way Dickens may describe the way human beings felt at Christmas emerge as the "Carol Philosophy."

It seemed that Charles Dickens name had end up linked with Christmas itself. When one little woman in London heard of Dickens death she became so worried that she changed into afraid that Santa Claus may want to die as properly.

'Dealings with the Firm of Dombey and Son' (1846 to 1848) – As stated in advance than this emerge as posted starting in October 1846 to April 1848 however in monthly problems. The novel come to be in the long run posted in a book form for purchase in 1848, and it centers on how commercial agency and its techniques could have an effect on a own family's rate variety.

'David Copperfield' (1849 to 1850) – It occurred to be the primary via Dickens like this type: Nobody had ever written about a person that discovered him round each day of his lifestyles. He protected this from May 1849 through November 1850, in month-to-month installments and then posted as a whole novel November 1850.

'Bleak House' (1852 to 1853) – After Dickens' daughter and his father died, and he separated from his partner, it appeared all his novels that observed commenced out expressing what appeared like a dark view of the world. In "Bleak House," he published a few installments that ran from 1852 to 1853 wherein he offers with British society and their hypocrisy. It changed into deemed to be Dickens' most complicated novel he had written to that issue in time.

'Hard Times' (1854) - The ebook takes location within the path of the height of what emerge as considered economic boom. Dickens' published it in 1854 and the e-book seems to consciousness on what the shortcomings of the employers are however furthermore people who are searching out the change.

'A Tale of Two Cities' (1859) – It regarded in 1859 that Dickens came out of that "dark novel" section whilst he published this ancient novel which befell at some point of the French Revolution in London and Paris. He allotted this novel in a periodical he had based totally, "All the Year Round."

In this historic novel, he focuses the tale on the subjects of the need for sacrifice and what the battle have become some of the inherent evils in revolution and oppression, and what the opportunity became of rebirth and resurrection.

'Great Expectations' (1861) - it too emerge as posted in its serial form among December 1860 through August 1861 and then produced in a singular shape in October 1861 have become taken into consideration to be Dickens' most huge accomplishment literarily.

The tale itself is wherein Dickens narrated inside the first person and focuses on the complete existence journeys of the moral development for Dickens protagonist which became an orphan named Pip. By using colorful characters and excessive imagery, the novel's subjects which have been so well obtained protected poverty, wealth, rejection, love, and evil instead of appropriate.

DICKENS' OTHER NOVELS

After "Oliver Twist" have been posted, Dickens tried to offer you with a healthful at the least to the quantity of its fulfillment. From 1838 till 1841, he issued "The Life and

Adventures of Nicholas Nickleby," "The Old Curiosity Shop" and "Barnaby Rudge."

There became some other novel that Dickens wrote inside the route of his "darkish length" with the aid of the choice of "Little Dorrit" (1857), that served as a fictional study of wherein and the manner human values can come into battle with all of the international's brutality.

Dickens' one novel "Our Mutual Friend," come to be additionally published in serial form in the route of and between 1864 thru 1865 earlier than it become released inside the whole shape of a e-book in 1865 and it analyzes London society and the way it has been impacted by way of using wealth and psychology.

"DARK" NOVELS

It seemed normal that the 1850s have been a dark and sad time for Dickens. Then in 1851, inner 14 days, Dickens's Dad and later absolutely actually one among his daughters died. But in 1858, he fell in love with an actress and separated from his first partner.

Chapter 4: Dickens In America

An idea, like a ghost, must be spoken to a hint earlier than it's going to explain itself.

Charles Dickens

Some of Charles Dickens travels have been distant places, and that they severa as to the period of stay. It appeared he cherished his trips anywhere he went. He felt it gave him extra references to his writing.

While however married to Catherine, Charles Dickens and his associate in 1842 traveled to america. When they again from this voyage, Charles started out writing his American notes for the "General Circulation" which changed into a sarcastic critique of the American materialism and their manner of lifestyles.

During the same time, it is felt he additionally had written "The Life and Adventures of Martin Chuzzlewit," which was the story approximately how the guys's struggle in survival in the ruthless American frontier.

It became in the course of this identical excursion that Dickens made his opinion identified about how plenty he hostile slavery and suggested all people of techniques plenty he supported the reform. He held lectures that he started out in Virginia and wound up in Missouri. This installation of lectures were attended so distinctly with its substantially big audiences, that fee tag scalpers may collect at the outer edges of his sports. It modified into Biographer J.B. Priestly that had written in the course of the excursion that Dickens appeared to experience "the nice welcome more than everyone else visiting America had ever obtained."

Dickens bragged that everybody seemed to flock spherical him like he had been an idol, however he end up a show-off. At first, Dickens cherished all the attention, however should ultimately resent all of the invasion of his privacy. He have emerge as aggravated approximately the way Americans crude and really social conduct as he might speak approximately later in his American Notes.

It made the Americans angry with him due to the truth Charles Dickens had criticized them plenty in the course of the number one tour in the US, he decided to launch a few different, 2d excursion within the U.S. It may final for a yr, and Dickens hoped to make topics proper with the us.

During his time inside the United States, Dickens did make a speech with a compelling charm that praised the entire United States inside the reprints of "American Notes for General Circulation" and "The Life and Adventures of Martin Chuzzlewit."

Dickens seventy-5 readings on the equal time as in the United States netted an anticipated $95,000 that in the Victorian generation, should amount to approximately $1.Five million nowadays in U.S. Greenbacks.

When Dickens arrived lower lower back home in London, he become so famous that the humans in London all identified him even as he might likely walk via the metropolis, accumulating any observations he may need to use as notion in his future paintings.

Dickens went to Italy and stayed for a big quantity of time, and this resulted inner the adventure software "Pictures from Italy" in 1846.

SOME SHOCKING TRUTHS ABOUT ENGLAND

Little Red Riding Hood have become my old flame. I felt that if I might also moreover want to have married Little Red Riding Hood, I need to have known satisfactory bliss.

Charles Dickens

During the middle part of the 19th century, the common existence span for citizens of London have end up 27 years vintage. If you have got been a part of the strolling elegance, your variety dropped all the manner right all the way down to 22 years.

A CHRISTMAS CAROL

It come to be posted in 1843 and simply so occurred it turned into the same year the first ever Christmas card modified into mailed, so it became out to be one of the very maximum well-known books all the time. It have been adapted extra times than one that can depend for display and degree, which protected the exquisite and the extraordinary movie version in 1951 that made Ebenezer Scrooge so famous. You also can need to discover any of its adaptions that would variety from plays to ballets and some of the present day Muppet classics. Oddly sufficient that the story following Scrooge while he begins recapturing the optimism and generosity of his more youthful days has stood the take a look at of a long time.

Almost 1/2 the funerals held in London were being held for youngsters which have been greater more youthful than ten years antique in 1839. Most of them had been dying from malnutrition or some contagion. Then in 1847, as a minimum a 1/2 million Londoners, approximately one-fourth of the London population, changed into tormented by typhus which changed into generally because of the sanitation problems.

RED RIDING HOOD

Charles Dickens felt that his first authentic love have grow to be "Little Red Riding Hood," who become, as all of us preferred, of course, the normal harmless that turn out to be approximately to be eaten through the sudden evil forces. Dickens cherished the story and felt that if he should or could have been allowed to marry Little Red Riding Hood his existence might have been lived in best bliss. In truth, his actual love life had been complete of all of the twists and bad selections.

It was not something unusual for children ages 6 or 7 to have jobs that they worked at the whole time. So many kids that lived outside London worked everyday hauling coal that they used for gas all through the Industrial Revolution.

What little schooling that Dickens did have as a teenagers had ended by the time he have turn out to be fifteen years antique while his Dad couldn't offer you with training. He did get what grow to be considered a low-stage interest in a crook corporation as a junior clerk. Dickens have become by no means sympathetic in any manner towards felony professionals, Charles did pass a bargain of his time at his task specific his co-human beings through mimicking after which losing the pits of cherries down on the tops of hats of the human beings strolling down on the street below the window.

It became no time earlier than Dickens had mastered shorthand, and this ability need to assist him in his writing immensely later in his lifestyles. When he started running as a reporter, he blanketed Parliament.

With the Victorian age, came the above regular moral tone. In the 1851 census, it did screen that as a minimum one-0.33 of the populace of England had never before set a foot interior a church.

Dickens and whilst he did fall in love with Catherine, the daughter of virtually one of London's newspaper editors modified right into a large deal at that factor. It became now not lengthy once they married that for some bizarre cause they decided to deliver Catherine's more youthful sixteen-year-vintage sister thru the call of Mary.

It seems through all payments that in the primary part of their married existence they were happy. When Catherine become pregnant with infant amount in 1837, Mary fell useless of coronary coronary heart failure.

Dickens felt that Mary have become the perfect example of innocence and goodness that become snatched away with the aid of some shape of random evil, possibly due to his self-proclamation of vintage flame who end up the further harmless Red Riding Hood.

Dickens fell virtually aside in his grief and commenced sporting a lock of Mary's hair. Dickens saved all of Mary's garments and may spend hours simply observing them. He even went to date to make funeral arrangements to have himself be buried subsequent to Mary while he died.

It makes one marvel what Catherine notion about Charles obsessive behavior. Catherine, it seemed had little or no time for thinking about due to the fact Dickens then invited her sister, Georgina, to live of their family. As their own family saved developing their marriage eroded due to the reality Dickens targeted on Catherine due to the fact the supply of his fury.

There are some claims that do have evidence this is quite convincing that at the same time as Dickens hung out with Ellen, that she even gave begin to a little one who died. Then there are others who attempt to mention that they never had any bodily courting. Fred Kaplan tells that Dickens modified into one who had pretty some sexual participants of the circle of relatives for maximum of his adulthood. There have turn out to be no longer a risk he might deny himself this pleasure even as he felt so in love with a more youthful female so attractive.

It is notion that Charles Dickens did buy homes for Ternan, then they traveled to France together, and stored a close courting collectively along with her until he died.

There changed into a 2013 movie "The Invisible Woman" that advised the tale in their longtime affair.

Hanging with the useful resource of the neck with a rope until one changed into dead had been quite common, and that they have been extensively attended. When Dickens have turn out to be a child, there had been over 220 crimes that might be punished via manner of dying. The infractions can be from homicide all the way to highway theft to the stealing of 5 shillings from a forgery, keep, and the maximum bizarre, the harmful of the Westminster Bridge.

Chapter 5: Close Brush With Death

It opens the lungs, washes the countenance, carrying sports the eyes, and softens down the mood; so cry away.

Charles Dickens

June ninth, 1865 have grow to be the nearest brush with loss of lifestyles that Dickens ever had in his lifestyles. He grow to be fortunate to have really survived, while others were now not that lucky. There have been forty to fifty injured, and ten people misplaced their lives in what got here to be referred to as the Staplehurst railway accident.

The day started out like a few extraordinary day. Charles, Ellen Ternan and her Ternan's mother had been coming back from Paris in the equal educate.

Near Staplehurst, the educate tune changed into being labored on, and the guys running on it had now not signaled to any of the oncoming trains that there might be a gap of 42 feet extended, inside the railroad tracks that led over the bridge.

The engineer of the teach noticed the trouble, but at the final minute, however it have emerge as too overdue for all people. The momentum by myself kept sporting the large engine and the first part of that train during the 40 -foot breach. It did not rely, the coaches at the rear and the center of the educate all fell into the river underneath, and all but one of those super coaches fell into that equal ravine. The educate that stayed at the rail emerge as the one that become occupied by using way of Mrs. Ternan, Ellen Ternan, and Dickens.

Their educate turn out to be now not one which fell into the river, but it become left placing from the bridge at an oddly steep mind-set. While Mrs. Ternan and Dickens have been no longer injured, Ellen only suffered minor accidents.

Dickens worked to get the Ternans out of the educate and then helped along with his fellow passengers. He recovered a bottle of brandy from off the educate and his top hat. He would fill his pinnacle hat with water and be doing some thing he need to to assist consolation and useful resource the injured. Dickens later defined the complete scene as some factor unattainable.

There took place to be one guy that grow to be seen for rescuers to appearance, but no man or woman ought to get to him and assist him get away. Still being pinned underneath the teach, that man later died. There isn't any concept of the ache and struggling he went through. At one time at some degree inside the rescue efforts, Dickens stopped for an injured girl who have been laid under a tree and gave her a sip of brandy. The next time Dickens exceeded thru her, she had died. Dickens worked for three hours doing everything he may also want to to assist lessen the ache of folks that had been suffering.

When rescuers ultimately arrived on the scene, and it become being evacuated, Dickens came about to recollect a few factor. He needed to get once more to his educate automobile to retrieve a few aspect he felt he wanted. He went over again into the teach vehicle another time to get his extremely-modern segment of "Our Mutual Friend," which modified into the novel he have been running on at the time.

It occurred that for years after this accident that Dickens could have surprising assaults of hysteria whilst he needed to journey through the usage of educate. Probably what we might are looking for advice from as "Panic Attacks" or even "Post Traumatic Stress Disorder" nowadays.

Dickens wrote in his postscript for "Our Mutual Friend":

June the 9th, Mr. And Mrs. Boffin (have been receiving Mr. And Mrs. Lammie for breakfast) and that they've been the usage of the South Eastern Railway on the identical time as I, had been in a harmful coincidence. After I had accomplished all I need to do in supporting others, I went lower lower back and climbed internal my educate instruct, however felt like I nearly have become over the bridge, then helped extricate this well worth couple. They had been dirty, but in any other case, they got here away unharmed. It become the same suitable end end result for Miss Bella Wilfer on her marriage ceremony day and a Mr. Riderhood who changed into examining Bradley Headstone's neckerchief while he lay slumbering. I can bear in mind feeling non secular thankfulness that I modified into in no way so close to loss of existence and not being a part of the readers lives all the time than I emerge as sooner or later of this time.

DICKENS AND SOME OF HIS WOMEN

A loving coronary heart is the truest know-how.

Charles Dickens

Dickens desired being found, but at the equal time, he have come to be a private character and in no way desired anyone to recognize a few element about his private life. That is why in 1860 whilst his marriage to Catherine had damaged up that he burned all his correspondence so, after his death, every time that could be, no person have to go through it an apprehend extra about his private existence than he favored them to apprehend.

Most experience that his intercourse life have end up trivial. To this creator, it does no longer seem that manner at the same time as you observed of the girls he have become involved with, and he managed to maintain mystery. Some historians say he become still a virgin at the same time as he married Catherine Hogarth at the same time as he come to be 24 years vintage. This creator unearths all of this difficult to believe.

Before that, he had continuously been in love or infatuated with one girl or a few one of a kind. The remaining infatuation stayed with him for 4 years. When the relationship did spoil off, Charles felt his coronary coronary heart might in no way be the equal.

It regarded whilst he have become concerned with Catherine Hogarth; he felt lots much less charged romantically. What can one say, she grow to be the boss's daughter with the useful resource of the way. When he met Catherine, he moreover met her younger sisters, little Mary who've turn out to be fourteen and Georgina who become six.

History says that the sisters all have turn out to be a number one a part of his life, but this author begs to differ. It appears the oddest of all of the relationships have come to be that together together with his younger sister-in-law Mary who emerge as fourteen at the time that he have become so enamored. She regarded to be the real love-of-his-life and belief for a few famous books.

Charles and Mary had usually gotten along well even in some unspecified time within the destiny of Charles and Catherine's dating days, but even now it's miles very terrific that his sister-in-law of 16 years vintage may flow into in with them as quickly due to the fact the newlyweds were given once more from their honeymoon.

Dickens did not seem like afflicted to profess how he pleased in her presence. And Mary cherished her brother-in-law. Mary left for a fast at the same time as however came yet again fast after Catherine had her first infant.

Dickens become turning into extra in name for than ever, and his works have been selling so nicely that they moved into a more grand fame quo on Doughty Street. Mary moved with them, and so did Charles more younger brother Fred.

A month later, Catherine, Dickens, and Mary all went to the theatre together to look a play that Dickens had written,

"Is She His Wife?"

When they arrived once more home, Mary and Charles sat up and talked until 1:00 a.M.

Mary went to her bedroom however have end up noticeably ill. They sent for the scientific medical doctors. Dickens have become the only who comforted her, waiting beside her until her fever would probably damage. After many hours of him preserving her in his fingers, she died.

Dickens have end up a shattered man. When it dawned on Dickens that she changed into vain, he took a ring off truly one in each of her hands that he wore on his for the rest of his days. He changed into given a lock of Mary's hair that he always saved with him as properly.

Dickens have grow to be fairly greatly surprised at the same time as Mary died so all of sudden, however there was a few component so ordinary via his reaction to the loss of lifestyles. It appeared his reaction made it enjoy like he would possibly have faster had someone else of their family died, however when you marvel who it'd were, feels a little alarming. Sometimes his words had been those of a determine bereaving, but he didn't act some issue like this at the same time as he later out of location of his personal youngsters.

Charles modified into happy that she had died in his fingers and no man or woman else together with her final terms have been whispered to and approximately him. He felt that there has been never another creature that become so great that ever breathed.

Dickens turn out to be 25 whilst Mary died, and it regarded he in no manner recovered from her dying. For the nice and the primary time in his existence, he truely surrender running. He did not turn in any new installments of Oliver Twist or Pickwick Papers. Rumors abounded.

When he started out going for walks once more on Oliver Twist, he determined out he couldn't kill off his person modeled after Mary, Rose Maylie, Oliver's teenage aunt, so adorable and pure; so moderate and mild, the way Rose lived.

Mary is seen all over again within the Dickens person of Agnes inside the e-book David Copperfield. Mary all of the time fixed Dickens concept of what a actual female must be, and that grow to be a young lady. To him, her age of 16 became whilst a female have become the most best: she come to be now not fat, nor worn-out, tedious, or dull.

It makes one surprise that what with Dickens had been positioned thru as a younger boy that it arrested his development. That someplace deep internal he had a thriller he had made high pleasant stayed alive, a model of a twelve-yr-old boy and Mary seemed to be the boy's fable of 1 that have grow to be being cared for and cherished.

John Forster, Dickens' friend, is the most effective that suggested him that in his memories 'Nell' needed to die. He argued with Dickens that Nell deserved a better destiny than a few different glad ending Dickens satisfied however nearly observed himself incapable of committing the deed.

After considered one of his books were published, Dickens had deliberate to visit America. But, an occasion got here up that harm him more than anybody could be capable of deliver an purpose of. Catherine's grandmother died and as she have become loss of life advocated every body she preferred to be buried subsequent to little Mary inside the Cemetery at Kensal Green. Dickens had usually planned on being married next to Mary. It changed proper into a devastating blow to him that he must no longer be mendacity subsequent to Mary after his demise.

After the grandmother's burial, Dickens locked himself away for three days due to the reality he became so distraught over now not being able to be buried subsequent to Mary.

Dickens went on a journey to America, and it modified proper right into a wonderful success. His first idea came right out of his mouth to Forster changed into approximately Mary. He knowledgeable him how he wished she is probably there with him.

Catherine did no longer have a danger in opposition with all and sundry that end up immortal.

Dickens have become an increasing number of pressured. His most modern-day e-book have emerge as not a fulfillment and Dickens favored to go away England once more.

Now he moved his family to the Italian City of Genoa in which it have become quiet. Not lengthy after moving there, Mary started vividly coming to him in his desires. Dickens knew as fast as he noticed her image that it turned into the spirit of Mary and the entire revel in changed into 'whole of sorrow and compassion for him.' He went on to confess that it lessen him to his coronary coronary heart and whilst he would awaken he might be sobbing.

He felt a decided want for girl recovery that he had always decided in Mary – but due to the truth that her lack of lifestyles, it had eluded him, irrespective of how well-known he became. His emotions for his partner Catherine had been getting an increasing number of horrible.

Until the day that Dickens died, he may need to in no way stop thinking about Mary. In the remaining three hundred and sixty five days he lived; he wrote that Mary end up in his mind all the time and turn out to be lots more even as he end up a fulfillment and had prospered at a few detail, and remembering her changed into an important part of his life, and as essential as his beating coronary coronary heart.

During 1860 Dickens changed into but seeking to come to terms collectively together with his separation from his ex-partner Catherine and approximately his dating that have become taking area with Ellen.

In July of 1860 Dickens, daughter, Katie, that he changed into closest to, had been given married and left their domestic on Gad's Hill. It turn out to be barely ten days after Katie's wedding that Charle's brother, Alfred died. And, as though that changed into not sufficient, Dickens' mom had emerge as senile and had to have constant looking. It could have been all of this together that have become the inducement at the back of Dickens in searching for to cast off his demons from the past.

On the day Dickens took his deep dive into despair it modified into difficult to apprehend the incentive, but it'd have helped to understand why within the global he determined to burn the letters he had from specific famous authors like George Eliot, Wilkie Collins, and William Makepeace Thackeray.

Plorn and Henry, the 2 youngest sons of Dickens, carried their Dad's baskets upon baskets of letters and fed them into the large fireplace. Dickens' daughter Mamie begged him time and again to reconsider what he end up doing and at least save a number of the letters.

It did now not depend wide variety wide variety to Dickens; he have become definitely decided to finish the venture he had started out. Just as they were finishing the burning, it commenced raining. Dickens stated that

"His correspondence of overcasting the face of the Heavens above."

PLAGUED BY COPYRIGHT

There are books of which the backs and covers are via a long manner the notable additives.

Charles Dickens

In January 1842 Charles Dickens grow to be traveling in the United States. During this ride, he spoke hundreds approximately the want for copyright agreements being wanted internationally. By the dearth of getting an settlement of such, it have end up allowing the appearance of his books just so they will be posted in the United States with none royalties being paid him without his permission.

The hassle affected the American writers too like Edgar Allan Poe. Poe's works were being posted over in England without his consent.

When Dickens first determined out he turned into losing money and it come to be because of no longer having any global copyright legal guidelines at some stage in 1837 in the path of the time that "The Pickwick Papers" which have been being published in any ebook shape. There have been times the radical could be reprinted and did no longer get his permission, and there have been instances they were imitated.

Dickens' struggles approximately the copyright laws started out to make it into a part of his fiction. There became a scene from Nicholas Nickleby in which Nicholas became talking with a person

"who dramatized throughout his time the whole of hundred 40-seven novels as speedy and as rapid as they had been posted, a few even quicker than they had been posted."

Authors could stay conscious thinking about the final word they'd written, even again weeks in the past. And, with out that author's permission, some different author might come alongside and put up even most effective a pamphlet the use of the real author's phrases, pull some garbled extract from the proper works of the authentic writer without giving him/her the acclaim they deserve. It is just like the distinction of pilfering or deciding on a person's pocket out in the street.

Chapter 6: Mesmerism

We forget the chains we put on in existence.

Charles Dickens

The illustrator that Dickens used for his e book, "A Christmas Carol," John Leech have turn out to be in an twist of destiny in 1849. It left John with the scenario that had signs and symptoms masses like a concussion and could not disappear regardless of what all of the medical scientific medical doctors he visited attempted to do to treatment it.

Leech suffered from pretty a few ache and feature become by no means capable of relaxation. When Dickens heard approximately the accident, he rushed rapid to the useful useful resource of his friend. In a bear in mind of days, Leech was superior extensively. What grow to be it that Charles Dickens modified into capable of do that all the medical clinical doctors had no longer been capable of do.

The story is going that Dickens had been able to assist Leech, his friend with the resource of the usage of mesmerism.

Franz Anton Mesmer superior Mesmerism via using hypnotic trances to heal others. Today we call Mesmerism "hypnosis" or the electricity of idea. It is utilized by a few psychiatrists in treating their patients.

During 1838 Charles Dickens attended plenty of lectures on mesmerism, and some were by using using John Elliotson.

Elliotson occurred to be the professor of medication that had delivered the number one stethoscope to England. He have become a professor that campaigned closer to all corrupt clinical practices.

Even even though Elliotson had many accomplishments, he was subsidized against the wall and compelled to surrender the training spot he had held for goodbye because of the scandal concerning his involvement with mesmerism in 1839.

It did now not recall to Dickens about all of the controversy; he changed into despite the fact that a believer in mesmerism. The reality come to be that Elliotson had taught Dickens the method and all people might probably speedy understand how skilled Dickens have become in this vicinity.

In the start, Charles Dickens became able to mesmerize his pals and family for a laugh and to assist with notable mother and father minor ailments. It become in 1844 on the identical time as Dickens took a take a look at a more tough case, the only of Madame de los angeles Rue.

She regarded to be through intense tension. It changed into extraordinarily profound. So lots that it triggered her to show off facial spasms and tics. Charles Dickens appeared beforehand to supporting and for the subsequent few months he is probably treating her regularly.

It grew to come to be out that the treatments labored. Within a month, Madame de l. A. Rue had made some of development. Madame de l. A. Rue had started out sound asleep at night time, and you may inform with the aid of the usage of looking at her that she changed into extra comfortable.

After the bodily signs and symptoms and signs and symptoms let up for Madame de la Rue, it became Dickens that began getting more inquisitive about what the real motive is probably.

The in addition the training persevered, the extra they started out out to awareness on de l. A. Rue's hallucinations, mind, and dreams. She commenced speakme about being chased via using using some "phantom." It seemed like their durations have been turning into like the ones of a affected man or woman with their therapist.

Dickens' partner at the time have become Catherine, and she or he or he became starting to emerge as very upset with all of the 'training' and Charles Dickens' 'fascination' with Madame de l. A. Rue.

By now, I am superb each person would love to apprehend how mesmerism works. Maybe it acted like a tranquilizer and taken on one to relaxation. It is shape of difficult to say. It seems bizarre that the fitness of de l. A. Rue and Leech each advanced once they were treated with the beneficial resource of Charles Dickens.

DEATH OF THE CHARLES DICKENS ERA

I first-rate ask to be free. The butterflies are unfastened.

Charles Dickens

Charles Dickens' lifestyles ended quickly after he had collapsed from a stroke at the equal time as he modified into consuming with Georgina Hogarth, his sister-in-law at his home. It became a don't forget that inner 24 hours, that on June 9th, 1870, Charles Dickens come to be said useless.

Dickens worked difficult all of the time, and the call for from his readers made him art work more difficult to satisfy their expectancies. He brought on constant problems for himself on a private degree, and all of it collectively human beings felt is what added approximately him to go through the stroke that brought his death at such an early age.

You ought to tell that via 1850, Charle's fitness was already weakened and then alongside alongside along with his father's passing, his sister and daughter dying, the entirety have turn out to be a lot worse.

He changed into not buried as he had asked subsequent to Mary Hogarth, or maybe in the easy type grave, he had requested to be buried. It become all toward his goals, and they lay him to rest inside the region of Poets' Corner there in Westminster Abbey.

Charles desire had commonly been that on his lack of existence he is probably buried there on the Cathedral of Rochester, privately and no luxuries; however after his death, his frame have grow to be buried in the plot for "Corner of the Poets" of Westminster Abbey.

A 365 days before he died, Dickens had written a will wherein he had left precise commands as to how his fortune should be allotted, and that covered records for his company personnel.

"Dickens sympathized with the horrible, those who suffered, the oppressed; and along with his dying, there was considered one of England's exceptional that come to be out of location to our worldwide."

These have been the words engraved on his tombstone.

Oddly enough neither Ellen Ternan or Dickens' accomplice attended his funeral. There is, but, an entire lot hypothesis that Ellen Ternan may have participated within the funeral in some cowl. They left his grave open for 2 days so the masses of his fans, whether or no longer terrible or rich, must file beyond – which become fine proof of the strength he held to touching the hearts of any and absolutely everyone from peasant to student.

It regarded that in many methods, his demise marked the completing of the Victorian age. It did no longer count quantity because of the reality Queen Victoria remained as ruler for loads extra years. When readers look again on that point body, it's far in no way Queen Victoria they seem to bear in thoughts. It is in fact Pip, the best encountering a mysterious convict out in the marshes of Anglia.

To his fans, it have become David Copperfield who changed into fleeing his stepfather who changed into so evil and Nicholas Nickleby who have come to be coming across all of the horrors of a Yorkshire boarding faculty. It is the reality that Nell is dying, Nancy murdered, Miss Havisham residing forever, commonly dressed for a wedding day to return.

It is Tiny Tim and Ebenezer Scrooge, the Old Parent, and Phenomenon of the Infant, the dipsomaniacal Sairey Gamp, the Artful Dodger, the hapless Miss Flite, the obsessive Bradley Headstone, and the alternative 2,000 or more women, youngsters, and men that Dickens had created to the touch anybody's hearts and brighten days.

Chapter 7: The Start Of His Life

Charles Dickens was born on February 7, 1812, the kid of a clerk on the Navy Pay Office. His dad, John Dickens, continuously living past his way, have turn out to be despatched to jail for debt inside the Marshalsea in 1824. 12-three hundred and sixty five days-antique Charles modified into being despatched far from university and pressured to transport art work at a boot-blacking production facility making 6 shillings a week to assist guide their family.

This difficult enjoy strong a shadow over the modern-day, sensitive little boy that ended up being a specifying, enhancing revel in in his existence, he would possibly later say that he in reality confused "how I might have been so rapid stable away at that age."

This younger people poverty and feelings of desertion, despite the fact that unidentified to his readers until after his lack of existence, is probably a huge effect on Dickens' later perspectives on social reform and the arena he can also want to produce through his fiction writing.

Dickens ought to write a complete of fifteen huge books which includes, Oliver Twist, Bleak House, Great Expectations, A Tale of Two Cities, and, the only that have become his non-public preferred, David Copperfield. He will forever and ever be linked with the occasion of Christmas because of his Christmas Books, the wonderful-acknowledged being A Christmas Carol. Dickens likewise modified, and brought to, weekly journals Household Words and All the All Round. Close to very last years of his lifestyles, he took a adventure throughout Great Britain and the US of America, giving public readings of his works.

Charles Dickens passed away as an vintage man of 57, worn-out with paintings and excursion, on June 9th, 1870. He desired to be buried, without excitement, in a hint cemetery in Rochester, Kent, and but the Country might no longer allow it. He end up placed to rest in Poet's Corner, Westminster Abbey, the flowers from limitless mourners overrunning the open tomb. Amongst the more lovely arrangements had been severa easy clusters of wildflowers, blanketed in rags.

John Dickens, who had a growing circle of relatives and a Navy transfer to Somerset Home in London, started out to have monetary problems, as do so a number of us.

As referred to, Charles changed into sent out to transport artwork at Warren's Blacking manufacturing facility at the identical time as he modified into twelve years of age, gluing labels on pots of blacking (shoe polish) ten hours an afternoon, six days in step with week, for which he changed into paid a weekly income of six shillings, the majority of which modified into used to help assist the family. Right after Charles started out out paintings at the blacking manufacturing facility his dad modified into detained for cash debt and sent out to the Marshalsea debtor's prison in Southwark.

At this time, his circle of relatives blanketed Charles, the older sister Fanny, the more youthful brothers Alfred and Frederick, and the more youthful sister Letitia. Everybody aside from Charles and Fanny went to move stay inside the Marshalsea with their parents or caretakers. Fanny changed into boarding at the Royal Academy of Music, and Charles inside the starting lodged with a landlady in Camden Town in north London. This showed to be too extended of a walk every day to the blacking production unit and to his circle of relatives in the Marshalsea, so a area have become rented for him on Lant Street in Southwark near the prison.

Young Charles, who imagined maturing as a gentleman, determined these desires rushed running together with everyday boys on the blacking production unit and later wrote "It is splendid to me how I might have been so fast forged away at such an age." Dickens shared this unpleasant a part of his younger humans thru the story of David Copperfield even though no individual observed out it changed into autobiographical till related to the resource of biographer John Forster after Dickens' loss of life.

After John Dickens' debt have come to be paid and he became launched from jail he took pity on more youthful Charles and removed him from the blacking manufacturing facility.

His mom, no matter the reality that, changed into of the opinion that he wants to stay to preserve to deliver sales for the family. Years later Dickens would possibly write "I do no longer write resentfully or madly: for I recognise all of these things have collaborated to make me what I am: but I in no way ever in some time forgot, I in no manner ever will forget about, I in no way ever can forget about, that my mom grow to be heat for my being again."

Charles emerge as to boom his schooling and modified into despatched out to Wellington Home Academy which end up run by the use of the intense schoolmaster William Jones who Dickens referred to as "sincerely the maximum oblivious man I actually have ever had the leisure to apprehend." Charles should spend 2 years, aged 12-14, at Wellington Home earlier than circle of relatives financial troubles all over again stepped in and his education changed into speedy stopped. A lot of his tales at university, and the masters that taught there, may need to later discover their manner into his fiction.

The Law and Early Journalism

In early 1827, Charles Dickens began out out work as a regulation clerk with the organization of Ellis and Blackmore in Gray's Inn, London. He later relocated to every other regulation workout but after about 2 years inside the criminal business enterprise Dickens selected that the law moved too often, and he grew tired of it. He have been given an admission fee charge price ticket to the British Museum and haunted the library there analyzing every little issue he can also want to get. John Dickens, leaving the Navy Department with a touch pension, determined artwork as a reporter on the Mirror of Parliament.

Young Charles taught himself firsthand, and he found his dad into art work on the Mirror of Parliament as a parliamentary press reporter.

Charles had been surprised with the aid of the usage of way of the theatre because of the truth his kids and generally participated within the theatre to interrupt the uniformity of reporting on parliamentary procedures. He wrote to George Bartley, supervisor of the Covent Garden Theatre, in 1832 soliciting for for an audition, which he acquired. On the day of the audition Charles was sick with a awful bloodless and irritation of his face and surely ignored the appointment he had signed up for. He wrote to Bartley clarifying the illness and that he may need to look for any other audition next season. He can also later understand how close to he got here to a actually super type of existence.

While though strolling for the Mirror of Parliament Dickens furthermore ended up being a parliamentary press reporter for a cutting-edge paper, the True Sun. He commenced out writing narratives at the time of this time taken into consideration virtually considered one of which, A Supper at Poplar Walk, became released in Month-to-month Publication. Dickens changed into paid sincerely not some thing for the tale however changed into elated at the same time as he found it in print. In 1834 he became hired as a press reporter for the Early morning Chronicle. Dickens decided taking a adventure the duration and breadth of Britain as a press reporter to be thrilling artwork. The editors of the Early morning Chronicle noticed functionality in the younger press reporter and requested him to install writing a series of sketches of every day lifestyles in London. Quickly Dickens furthermore changed into writing sketches for different courses and papers.

And one of these become the Night Chronicle changed thru George Hogarth. Hogarth welcomed Dickens, who became 23 on the time, to his residence in Chelsea wherein he met, and become amazed and inspired with the useful resource of, Hogarth's nineteen-one year-vintage daughter Catherine. Love grow to be in the air.

Dickens, who emerge as writing feverishly, and shielding down the art work of a press reporter, now placed himself inside the throes of passion. He ended up being a everyday traveler to the Hogarth domestic and quick proposed marriage, which Catherine rapidly ordinary. They have been wed at St. Luke's church, Chelsea on April 2, 1836. And approximately 2 months former his series of narratives became released in e-book shape with the aid of John Macrone entitled Sketches through way of Boz with illustrations via famous artist George Cruikshank. Dickens' pseudonym Boz originated from his greater extra younger brother Augustus's via-the-nose pronunciation of his very personal label, Moses.

Chapter 8: His Earliest Novels

Charles and Catherine Dickens arranged the house obligations in Furnivall's Inn. Charles' brother Fred, Catherine's sister Mary, and a servant finished the residence chores and organized the own family.

In March 1836 Dickens started out writing a loose series of the reviews of a carrying membership entitled The Pickwick Documents. Released in normal monthly installations on the idea of his new publishers, Chapman and Hall, the appeal of the series skyrocketed, especially after the intro of Pickwick's servant, Samuel Weller, in monetary catastrophe 10. While Pickwick have come to be nevertheless being serialized, Dickens began out writing Oliver Twist, which emerged in weekly components within the ebook, Bentley's Miscellany.

On January sixth, 1837, Catherine and Charles celebrated the delivery of their first teen, Charles Jr, called Charley. In March the growing own family transferred to new quarters at forty eight Doughty Street. On May seventh, after participating in the theatre with Charles and Catherine, seventeen-three hundred and sixty five days-antique Mary ended up being sick. She have been given worse at a few stage in the night time and exceeded away the following day in Charles' hands.

The circle of relatives become distraught, and Charles the most out of all of them. He took a hoop from Mary's finger and wore it the rest of his existence. Mary lives again in Dickens' fiction within the person of some of his "splendid girls" together with Rose Maylie and Little Nell. Another of Catherine's sisters, whose call emerge as Georgina, ultimately took Mary's vicinity within the Dickens home.

While weekly episodes of Oliver Twist have been performing in Bentley's Miscellany, Dickens commenced normal monthly serialization of Nicholas Nickleby. To look into the story Dickens and his illustrator, Hablot Knight Browne (Phiz) made a adventure to Yorkshire, incognito, to look at the infamous boarding faculties there. After Nickleby, Dickens began out a weekly manual entitled Master Humphrey's Clock that featured, to call some memories, the tale of Little Nell and her grandpa referred to as The Old Interest Shop.

This story ended up being so well-known that it absolutely took manipulate of weekly versions of Master Humphrey's Clock to the exemption of all different writing. With the belief of The Old Interest Shop, Dickens right away began out out weekly e-book, additionally in Master Humphrey's Clock, of Barnaby Rudge.

After finishing Barnaby Rudge, Dickens selected to take a touch while off and advocated his publishers, Chapman and Hall, to boom him cash to make a journey to America, with the assure of a guidebook on go back. Charles and Catherine now had 4 kids: Charley (1837), daughters Mary (1838) and Katie (1839), and youngest little one Walter (1841). It come to be decided that the children ought to be left at domestic with Dickens' suitable friend, star William Macready and his marriage partner.

Charles and Catherine, similarly to Catherine's housemaid, Anne Brown, set sail aboard the steamship Britannia on January three, 1842 and landed at Boston on January 22. He changed into proper away subjected to the American emblem name of hero reward that rather perplexed him. He wrote domestic that "I can do honestly not something that I need to do, move in truth nowhere in which I want to move, and notice really not anything that I need to see. If I turn to the street, I'm accompanied through a plethora." Dickens' preliminary ardour grew to come to be to dissatisfaction due to the fact the journey of America dragged out. He have grow to be pestered in journalism for his ongoing harping at the problem of global copyright, originating from the clean truth that even though pretty well-known in the States, he have been given certainly now not something for his artwork presented there. Dickens' trips in America 1842. To Macready he wrote the following, "this isn't the republic I came to look; this is not the republic of my creativity."

Upon returning domestic he penned the promised guidebook, American Notes, a alternatively uncomplimentary description of America, and discovered that with Martin Chuzzlewit, released in monthly additives, wherein the lead character goes to America and undergoes the precise same shape of prolonged, mercenary humans Dickens determined there. The tale wasn't properly gotten and didn't promote properly. Neither had Barnaby Rudge, and Dickens felt that perhaps his moderate had headed out.

Dickens determined himself in alarming economic straits. He had acquired significantly from his publishers for the American journey he had made, and neither the promised guidebook, American Notes, nor Martin Chuzzlewit had sold thoroughly. Aside from this, his family went straight away to expand with their 5th infant, infant Francis, who emerge as approximately to go into into the region. His feckless dad modified into acquiring cash in Charles' name inside the back of his once more. He needed an concept for a latest e-book that might please his budgeting issues.

The seeds for the tale that ended up being A Christmas Carol were planted in Dickens' thoughts finally of a adventure to Manchester to speak in the beneficial useful resource of education. Thoughts of schooling as a solution for criminal interest and poverty, further to scenes he had sincerely presently professional on the Field Lane Ragged School, added on Dickens to cope with to "strike a sledgehammer blow" for the poor. As the concept for the tale took form and the writing began in earnest, Dickens ended up being fascinated in the ebook. He wrote that because the story saved unfolding, he "wept and chuckled, and wept another time' and also that he 'perambulated the black streets of London fifteen or twenty miles many a night on the identical time as all sober oldsters had long beyond to sleep." Dickens changed into honestly at odds with Chapman and Hall over the marginally low invoices from Martin Chuzzlewit and determined on to self-post the ebook, spending an excessive amount of on colour illustrations and rate binding and after that setting the fee low so that everybody also can need to govern it. The ebook turn out to be a direct fulfillment, however royalties were low after production costs were paid.

Serialization of Martin Chuzzlewit got here to a bring about July, 1844, and Dickens envisaged the concept of some one-of-a-kind guidebook; this time he may additionally need to go to Italy. The family spent a twelve months in Italy, to start with in Genoa, and after that taking a experience thru the southern a part of the nation. He wrote the second of his Christmas Books, The Chimes, at the equal time as in Genoa and despatched his studies domestic inside the form of letters that have been released in the Daily News. Those were accrued proper right into a single quantity entitled Images from Italy in May 1846.

Dickens accompanied the Italian adventure with the normal month-to-month serialization of Dombey and Child. The e-book became wonderful for being the number one where Dickens used notes he known as mems to place out the story in advance of time.

This brought about a higher arranged e-book and the completed ebook is a long way more cohesive than his former books had been. The e-book supplied well, and Dickens obtained a organization financial footing that would bring him the rest of his life.

Throughout the 1840s Dickens, with a performers of circle of relatives and friends in tow, started acting in newbie theatricals in London and throughout Britain. Charles labored relentlessly as celebrity and impresario and usually adjusted scenes, helped carpenters, superior garments, created playbills, and generally manipulate the whole production of the performances. The Dickens' newbie performers even accomplished times for Queen Victoria and Prince Albert.

Chapter 9: The Years Inside The Middle

In 1839 the Dickens family moved from Doughty Street to a larger home at Devonshire Balcony close to Regent's Park. The own family went right now to develop with the addition of sons Alfred (1845), Sydney (1847), and Henry (1849).

Dickens went on to jot down down a e-book for the Christmas season each yr. After A Christmas Carol (1843), and The Chimes (1844), he positioned with The Cricket at the Hearth (1845), The Fight of Life (1846), and The Haunted Man and the Ghost's Deal (1848). All of these provided properly on the time of ebook, however none continued as A Christmas Carol has.

Dickens had started out writing an autobiography inside the past due 1840s that he showed his right pal and destiny biographer, John Forster. He determined the writing too uncomfortable and burned what he had written. He decided as an opportunity to paintings his tale into the imaginary account of David Copperfield, which he later referred to as his personal desired among his books. That story modified into serialized from May 1849 till November 1850. Throughout the writing of Copperfield, the decided Dickens commenced out every other venture, a weekly ebook called Family Words. Charles worked as editor and contributor with added quantities supplied with the useful resource of means of diverse authors. Also, on the time of the writing of Copperfield Catherine added to lifestyles a toddler, known as for David Copperfield's accomplice Dora. Dora, sickly from begin, handed away at 8 months antique.

Dickens accompanied David Copperfield with what many hold in thoughts his work of paintings, Bleak Home. Dickens used his former experience as a court docket press reporter to inform the story of an extended case in the Courts of Chancery. At the time of the writing of Bleak Home Catherine brought to lifestyles a boy, Edward (1852), nicknamed Plorn. Edward might be final of Charles and Catherine's kids and the circle of relatives moved once more, this time to Tavistock Home. Following Bleak Home Dickens serialized his subsequent e-book, Hard Times, in his weekly e-book, Family Words. Following Hard Times Dickens went lower lower back to the unpleasant children memory of his dad's prison time for cash debt with the tale of Little Dorrit. Amy Dorrit's dad, William, grow to be a detainee within the Marshalsea debtor's prison and Amy was in truth born there.

Throughout the 1850s Charles and Catherine's marriage started out to reveal symptoms of problem. Dickens grew appreciably discontented with Catherine whom, after bringing to lifestyles 10 youngsters, had grown as a substitute stout and slow. She become notably not able to maintain up collectively collectively along with her lively companion. The trouble capped even as Dickens ended up being enthralled with a younger starlet, he met at some point of one of his beginner theatricals, Ellen Ternan. Charles and Catherine had been break up up in 1858 and brought about a public stir mainly brought to with the aid of way of Dickens' preference to exonerate himself. All of the Dickens youngsters, with exemption of Charley, would stay with their dad, as could Catherine's sister, Georgina. The courting with Ternan, the depth of which remains being discussed, would possibly keep the rest of Dickens' lifestyles.

Dickens and his kids had now moved into the property Gads Hill Place in Kent that he had acquired in 1856 close to his teenagers home of Chatham. As a younger boy, Dickens ought to walk with the aid of the use of the super home, constructed in 1780, with his dad who knowledgeable him that with exertion he should ultimately stay on this type of high-quality belongings. In 1864

Dickens were given, from superstar accurate pal Charles Fechter, a -story Swiss chalet that Dickens had installation across the roadway from Gads Hill with a tunnel below the roadway for get right of access to. Dickens wrote his last works in his research take a look at at the satisfactory floor of the chalet.

Alarmed at the abuse of the personal letters of public guys, and with some of tracks of his very own to cowl, Dickens burned every letter he had ever gotten in a bonfire at Gads Hill on September third, 1860 and quipped "Would to God every letter I had ever written end up on that stack."

The separation with Catherine moreover brought approximately a rift among Dickens and his publishers, Bradbury and Evans. Bradbury and Evans also launched the famous ebook Punch. When they refused to launch Dickens' non-public assertion, his cause of the modern separation, Charles raged and refused to have extra negotiations with them. He stopped guide of his weekly publication, Home Words, continuing it under a brand new name, All the All twelve months, and along along with his antique publishers, Chapman and Hall.

To guide earnings of the modern day weekly, Dickens decided on to release his subsequent 2 books, A Tale of Cities, and Great Expectations, in weekly installations in the ebook. For A Tale of two Cities Dickens used his appropriate buddy, Thomas Carlyle's History of the Reign Of Terror as a referral. The second of his 2 historic fictions, the primary being Barnaby Rudge, many felt that the ancient precision of the e-book added to the as an alternative un-Dickensian experience of the story.

Chapter 10: The Late Years

Somewhere in May 1864, Dickens commenced book of what might be his last finished ebook. Released in everyday monthly installations, Our Mutual Friend touches the familiar theme of the evils and corruption that the affection of coins brings. Experiencing the starter days of health trouble that would afflict him the relaxation of his lifestyles, Dickens located the writing difficult; the regular monthly installations did not sell well regardless of a large advertising blitz. On the ninth of June 1865, taking a experience again from France with Ellen Ternan and her mother, and with the modern-day set up of Our Mutual Friend, the train in which they were taking a journey grow to be related to a mishap in Staplehurst, Kent. Most have been killed however Dickens and his friends were given away excessive damage even though Dickens stated in some time that he felt "as an alternative shattered and separated" and later skilled "dubious hurries of horror" even the usage of in hansom taxis.

In the overdue 1850s Dickens started out out to contemplate a 2nd test out to America, lured with the useful resource of the cash he should make with the aid of way of extending his public readings there. Regardless of pleas no longer to go from circle of relatives and friends surely due to often illness, he finally selected to head and seemed in Boston on November 19, 1867. The real plan required a test out to Chicago and as a protracted way west as St. Louis. Just because of sickness and terrible climate this concept have become ditched, and Dickens did not organization from the northeastern states. He remained for 5 months and gave seventy six pretty famous performances for which he earned, after charges, an terrific $one hundred forty,000.

At a supper in his honor in New York on April 18, 1868, Dickens, citing awful elements of the 1842 experience, stated that each he and America had prolonged past through notable exchange for the motive that point of his last go to.

He stated some component about the first rate treatment he had gotten from anyone he had encounter on this journey and swore to embody a assertion imagined to relieve any tensions as an appendix to each duplicate of the two books in which he describes America (American Notes and Martin Chuzzlewit).

Dickens lower returned domestic in May, 1868, as an possibility rejuvenated on the time of the ocean adventure, to a complete load of hard work. He proper away plunged once more into enhancing All the All year and, in October, started out out a very good-bye analyzing experience of Britain that protected a state-of-the-art, virtually enthusiastic and physically taxing, overall performance of the murder of Nancy from Oliver Twist.

Regular monthly manual of what changed into to be his very last e-book, The Secret of Edwin Drood, started out out in April 1870. On the night time time of June 8, 1870, Dickens, after operating at the contemporary installation of Drood that early morning in the chalet at Gads Hill, suffered a stroke and passed away the next day. The Secret of Edwin Drood have turn out to be precisely half of of finished, and the secret's unsolved to these days.

Dickens had preferred to be buried, without pleasure, in a bit cemetery in Rochester, however the Country could now not permit it. He turn out to be placed to rest in Poet's Corner, Westminster Abbey, the flowers from endless mourners overrunning the open tomb.

Chapter 11: "Our Mutual Friend" With The Resource Of Charles Dickens

Our Mutual Friend emerge as the fourteenth and closing finished e-book of Charles Dickens. He started out out writing it in 1863. It changed into earlier than the entirety launched in month-to-month installations that began out in May of 1864 and resulted in November 1865.

Marcus Stone emerge as the illustrator.

Our Mutual Friend-- Dickens's Life at The Time

On September twelfth, 1863 his mother, Elizabeth passes away.

In November of 1863 Dickens starts offevolved offevolved to put in writing Our Mutual Friend.

Walter Dickens, his child, passes away in India in January of 1864.

The first installation of Our Mutual Friend is released in May of 1864.

In June of 1865 Charles Dickens is associated with the Staplehurst train mishap.

The ultimate chapters of Our Mutual Friend are released in November of 1865.

The Staplehurst Train Mishap

In 1865, Charles Dickens had a broom with loss of life. While he persisted, others had been not as fortunate. 10 human beings surpassed away and 40 have been hurt in the Staplehurst educate mishap.

On June 9th of 1865, Charles have grow to be coming back from a adventure to Paris. In the train with him had been Ellen Ternan and her mother.

The teach tune have end up being regular near Staplehurst. There become a forty foot long vicinity in the tracks over the bridge crossing the River Beult. The educate's engineer diagnosed the trouble at the final minute. However, it modified into a protracted manner too late.

The engine and the number one a part of the train made it throughout the distance. Even so, the coaches inside the center and the lower back of the educate fell right now into the river mattress. All however one of the exceptional coaches entered into the gorge. That come to be the instruct that delivered Dickens and the Ternans.

When the mishap scene modified into being left, Dickens recalled some component. He made his way again into the damaged train one very last time to gain the current installation of Our Mutual Friend, the e book he changed into writing on the time.

We'll Never Really Know

In Our Mutual Friend one of the characters is taken into consideration to be lifeless, however in reality isn't always. In The Secret of Edwin Drood, Dickens's remaining e-book, Edwin Drood vanishes. Was Drood killed? People accept as true with so however no character is ever located.

Was Dickens making plans to apply the exact equal plot twist that he 'd utilized in Our Mutual Friend? Maybe, just like the man or woman in Our Shared Buddy, Edwin Drood became now not definitely useless. We'll in no way ever understand. Dickens exceeded away in advance than The Secret of Edwin Drood became finished.

Dust Business

The dirt, or trash, commercial enterprise plays a very large factor in Our Mutual Friend

The older John Harmon made his fortune as a dust expert. Noddy Boffin in the end finally ends up being the "Golden Dustman" at the identical time as Silas Wegg exhibits a few difficulty in a mound of trash that he thinks may additionally need to remove Noddy's wealth.

In the mid-19th century, trash became amassed through using private experts. The garbage became stacked into mounds and people sorted through the mounds looking for things to promote. They may additionally find out style jewelry or cash that changed into with the useful resource of risk discarded.

Yet, the bulk of the garbage became offered as primary materials for special markets. Soap makers, roadway contractors, paper makers, and others bought merchandise from dust experts.

Themes in Our Mutual Friend

One of the not unusual subjects of the e-book is the corruption that wealth can supply. Bella Wilfer goes via extraordinary changes at a few degree within the ebook as she handles this trouble. Towards the start of the ebook, she makes a sensational announcement.

"I even have now made up my mind that I need to have coins, Pa. I sense that I cannot ask it, acquire it, or take or thieve it; and so, I even have regular that I want to marry it." Later inside the ebook, her emotions exchange. "O Mr. Rokesmith, in advance than you skip, if you can however make me terrible all over again! O! Make me terrible over again, Someone, I plead and pray, or my coronary coronary heart will spoil if that is taking place! Pa, pricey, make me terrible all once more and take me home! I became terrible enough there, but I had been so much even worse right right here. Do now not supply me cash, Mr. Boffin, I will now not have coins. Keep it from me, and incredible allow me talk to particular little Pa, and lay my head on his shoulder, and inform him all my sorrows. No one else can apprehend me, no man or woman else can consolation me, no individual else is aware of how no longer well worth I am, and however can in reality love me like a infant. I'm better with Pa than every body-- greater innocent, extra sorry, extra glad!" Characters in Our Mutual Friend Mr. Nicodemus "Noddy" Boffin labored for the senior Mr. Harmon. He and his associate obtained Old Mr. Harmon's fortune for the purpose that his little one and beneficiary, John Harmon, had manifestly exceeded away.

Boffin employs John Rokesmith (certainly John Harmon) to be his personal secretary.

Boffin pretends to come again lower back beneath the spell of his new wealth and acts in a parsimonious fashion. He fires John, however later it's far uncovered that this is all a part of a plan to test Bella's proper intents and values.

"Mrs. Boffin and me, ma'am, appear humans, and we do now not need to fake to something, nor but to head spherical and spherical at a few thing honestly because of the fact there is continuously a right now way to each little element." ~ Mr. Boffin Mrs. Henrietta Boffin is Mr. Boffin's partner.

Opening her eyes all yet again, and seeing her partner's face across the desk, she leaned ahead to present it a pat at the cheek, and took a seat to dinner, saying it to be the terrific face inside the international. ~ Description of Mrs. Boffin John Harmon is successor to the Harmon property. Even so, there can be a state of affairs. He wants to wed Bella Wilfer.

A frame became decided inside the Thames thru Gaffer Hexam and end up misidentified as John Harmon This offers John the threat to deal with each unique identity.

First, he is taking on the call of Julius Hanford. Then he sooner or later finally ends up being John Rokesmith.

Under the choice of John Rokesmith, John Harmon in the end ends up being a personal secretary for the Boffins.

John falls for Bella Wilfer and proposes marriage. Though, he's rebuffed as Bella wants to wed a rich man.

After John loses his popularity with Mr. Boffin, Bella alters her thoughts and that they wed.

The smooth fact comes out that John Rosesmith is without a doubt John Harmon.

"It is a feel no longer skilled with the useful resource of many mortals," said he, "to be finding out a churchyard on a wild windy night time time, and to feel that I no greater keep a area among the living than those vain do, or maybe to recognize that I lie buried some area else, as they lie buried right right here. Absolutely not whatever makes use of me to it. A spirit that turned into as soon as a guy must barely experience whole stranger or lonelier, going unacknowledged amongst humanity, than I revel in." ~ John Harmon.

Bradley Headstone is the schoolmaster of Charley Hexam Bradley fancies Charley's sister; Lizzie His advances are rebuffed. Headstone requires to stalking his competitor for Lizzie's love, Eugene Wrayburn.

Later Headstone attacks Wrayburn and leaves him for useless.

"You comprehend what I'm going to mention. I clearly love you. What wonderful men may suggest after they use that expression, I can not tell; what I mean is, that I'm under the effect of a few extremely good appeal which I even have withstood fruitless, and which overmasters me. You may additionally want to draw me to hearth, you can draw me to water, you can draw me to the gallows, you could draw me to any lack of life, you could draw me to a few component I clearly have maximum stayed far from, you may draw me to any direct exposure and shame. That and the confusion of my mind, in order that I'm in shape for honestly not anything, is what I suggest by means of the usage of your being the break of me. However, if you may pass lower back a notable option to my offer of myself in a marriage, you can draw me to any suitable-- every unique-- with same pressure. ~ Bradley Headstone speakme with Lizzie Hexam.

Charley Hexam is the child of Gaffer Hexam. Charley desires to grow to be being a schoolmaster and is caused in that mission by means of his sister, Lizzie.

" Do no longer pass announcing I in no way ever knew a mother," interposed the boy, "for I knew a chunk sister that turn out to be sister and mother each." ~ Charlie Hexam speakme about his sister Lizzie.

Jesse "Gaffer" Hexam is the dad of Lizzie and Charley.

Dickens at times describes Gaffer as "the fowl of sufferer" in Our Mutual Friend.

Gaffer works as a waterman who makes his dwelling thru locating and obtaining lifeless our our bodies from the Thames. He is the individual that well-knownshows the frame determined as John Harmon Lizzie Hexam is the daughter of Gaffer Hexam and the sister of Charley Hexam.

Lizzie resorts with Jenny Wren after the loss of lifestyles of her dad Later Lizzie receives away the place. She's trying to interrupt out the strain produced through Bradley Headstone and Eugene Wrayburn defending her love.

After Eugene is grievously harm, Lizzie weds him.

Mortimer Lightwood is a prison consultant and actual buddy of Eugene Wrayburn.

Pleasant Riderhood is the daughter of Rogue Riderhood. She works as a pawnbroker.

Roger "Rogue" Riderhood works as a waterman. Implicates Gaffer Hexam of killing John Harmon.

John Rokesmith-- See John Harmon.

Eugene Wrayburn is a prison expert and a outstanding friend of Mortimer Lightwood. Eugene falls for Lizzie Hexam.

Eugene is assaulted via the usage of Bradley Headstone, who's additionally intrigued with the aid of the use of Lizzie. Headstone leaves him for useless, but Eugene is placed and saved thru Lizzie. They wed.

Silas Wegg is hired to teach Mr. Boffin a way to take a look at.

Bella Wilfer changed into to be the associate of John Harmon. The Boffins took her in after John Harmon have become obviously drowned.

John Harmon, within the guise of John Rokesmith, proposes marriage. Bella refuses thinking about that she desires to wed a rich guy. Nevertheless, she adjustments her mind after Harmon loses his position with Mr. Boffin.

" I actually have comprised my mind that I ought to have coins, Pa. I sense that I cannot plead it, acquire it, or take it; and so I surely have consistent that I should wed it." ~ Bella speaking collectively collectively together with her dad.

Reginald "Rumty" Wilfer is Bella's dad.

" Well!" decided R. Wilfer, cheerfully, "cash and merchandise are really the high-quality of pointers." Jenny Wren's actual call is Fanny Cleaver. Jenny is handicapped and works as a fashion style designer for dolls. She gives along side her dad who she describes as her "awful youngster".

Chapter 12: A Christmas Carol With The Aid Of The Use Of The Usage Of Charles Dickens

A Christmas Carol, maximum in all likelihood the most famous piece of fiction that Charles Dickens ever wrote, became released in 1843.

The publisher modified into Chapman & Hall (even though Dickens paid the publishing charges) and the illustrator become John Leech.

Publication and Appeal of "A Christmas Carol"

Technically speaking, A Christmas Carol become launched with the aid of the usage of Chapman & Hall. Yet, in an interesting turn of sports activities, Dickens paid the publishing expenses himself.

Sales of Martin Chuzzlewit, furthermore launched with the aid of way of way of Chapman & Hall, had been hundreds a whole lot less than predicted. The owners of the agency started out to depression in the marketability of Dickens's art work. As a cease end result, they proposed that A Christmas Carol be launched in a low-rate series of Dickens's works or probably as a part of a ultra-modern guide.

Dickens have turn out to be decided that A Christmas Carol be launched as a pinnacle fantastic, stand-on my own e-book.

After a conversation some of the activities, they got here to an uncommon agreement.

Dickens would cash the manual of A Christmas Carol. He must get the earnings. Chapman & Hall can be paid for the printing fees and get a repaired fee on the number of copies sold.

Since Dickens modified into shopping for the publishing of the ebook, he wanted the e-book completed his manner. There have been problems with the color of the endpapers, the become aware of net page and the ebook binding.

A Christmas Carol modified into the first-rate ebook of the 1843 excursion. By Christmas it offered 6 thousand copies and it went at once to be famous into the stylish 365 days.

Unfortunately, A Christmas Carol changed into now not the moneymaker that Dickens was hoping it is probably. Sales were proper, however the e-book fees have been excessive.

The e-book is as well-known in recent times because it have emerge as over 175 years in the past. Charles Dickens, through the voice of Scrooge, keeps to advise us to honor Christmas in our hearts and try to preserve the whole thing all one year.

Rough Schools

Dickens have become associated with charities and social issues during his entire life. At the time that he wrote A Christmas Carol he have become definitely involved about impoverished kids who became to crook hobby and delinquency so you can go through.

Dickens, and moreover others, idea that education must provide a manner to a much better lifestyles for those children. The Ragged School movement located the ones mind into motion.

The faculties provided loose schooling for children inside the internal-town. The motion had been given its name from the manner the kids going to the college had been dressed. They generally wore scruffy or difficult clothes.

In September of 1843 Dickens went to the Field Lane Ragged School. In a letter to his accurate friend, Miss Coutts, he described what he located on the university:

I clearly have on and rancid seen, in all the weird and horrible subjects I in reality have visible in London and in one of a kind places something so stunning due to the fact the alarming neglect approximately about of soul and frame displayed in those children. And notwithstanding the truth that I apprehend; and am as wonderful as it's far feasible for one to be of something which has no longer befell; that in the prodigious struggling and lack of know-how of the swarming loads of humanity in England, the seeds of its certain lessen to rubble are planted.

Themes of A Christmas Carol thru way of Charles Dickens

Scrooge's change is famous. At the start of the story, he is a grasping, self-focused individual.

" Every moron who tackles with 'Merry Christmas' on his lips, need to be boiled along collectively with his personal pudding, and buried with a stake of holly through his heart." to the individual that "knew the way to keep Christmas nicely"

Scrooge is a penny pincher who shows a delegated absence of challenge for the relaxation of humanity. Nevertheless after a ghostly night time time, Scrooge sees existence in a whole new manner.

He ended up being as nicely an extremely good buddy, as actual a draw near, and as suitable a person, as the good vintage town knew, or each other proper vintage metropolis, city, or district, within the proper antique.

Dickens seems to be reminding us of the significance in paying attention to the lives of those round us.

" It is wanted of each man," the ghost once more, "that the spirit within him need to walk foreign places amongst his fellow-guys, and adventure anywhere; and, if that spirit goes now not forth in life, it is condemned to obtain this after loss of existence."

Dickens had this to say approximately A Christmas Carol:

I absolutely have endeavored in this Ghostly little ebook, to elevate the Ghost of a Concept, as a way to no longer positioned my readers out of humor with themselves, with each one-of-a-kind, with the season, or with me. May it hang-out their homes thankfully, and nobody dream to put it.

Their committed Good buddy and Servant,

C. D.

December, 1843

This listing of A Christmas Carol characters is demonstrated in alphabetical order.

Belle grow to be engaged to Scrooge at one time. She broke off the engagement on the equal time as she found a actual alternate in him.

" If you have got been unfastened to-day, to-morrow, the opportunity day, may even I trust that you can pick a dowerless lady--you who, on your in particular self-self belief collectively along with her, weigh every little factor with the useful resource of Gain: or, selecting her, if for a minute you have been wrong enough for your one supporting idea to carry out that, do I not realize that your repentance and regret may want to truly have a look at? I do; and I launch you. With a complete coronary coronary heart, for the affection of him you as quickly as were."--Belle breaking off her engagement to Scrooge

Bob Cratchit is Scrooge's employee and the dad of Tiny Tim Bob gives together together with his marriage partner and 6 children in a 4-room domestic.

Bob had however fifteen "Bob" a-week himself; he took on Saturdays but fifteen copies of his First call; and but the Ghost of Christmas Present blessed his four-roomed home!

Mrs. Cratchit is the companion of Bob Cratchit.

Oh, a exquisite pudding! Bob Cratchit said, and evenly too, that he seemed it because the top notch fulfillment attained through Mrs. Cratchit when you do not forget that their marriage. Mrs. Cratchit said that now the burden became off her thoughts, she might admit she had had her doubts approximately the quantity of flour. Everyone had a few component to mention approximately it, however no individual said or notion it end up at all a bit pudding for a massive circle of relatives. It ought to had been flat heresy to carry out that. Any Cratchit might've blushed to intend this shape of difficulty.

Martha Cratchit is the oldest daughter of Bob and Mrs. Cratchit. She works as a milliner.

Peter Cratchit is the oldest child of Bob and Mrs. Cratchit.

Tiny Tim Cratchit is the kid of Bob Cratchit, Scrooge's employees member. Tiny Tim is paralyzed.

Both the Ghost of Christmas Present and the Ghost of Christmas Yet to Come reveal that Tiny Tim's fitness problem is immoderate and he does now not have prolonged to stay.

" In some way he receives considerate, sitting with the resource of himself lots, and thinks the strangest stuff you ever heard. He informed me, getting domestic, that he was hoping the humans observed him within the church, just due to the fact he changed right into a cripple, and it could be interesting to them to recollect on Christmas Day, who made lame beggars walk, and blind men see." ~ Bob Cratchit speaking about Tiny Tim.

Fan have become Scrooge's extra younger sister and the mom of Fred.

" Always a sensitive being, whom a breath may also have withered," stated the Ghost. "But she had a pretty massive coronary coronary heart!"

Mr. Fezziwig-- When Scrooge grow to be young, he worked as Mr. Fizziwig's apprentice.

" He has the energy to render us glad or disillusioned; to make our business enterprise mild or difficult; an amusement or a work. Say that his electricity is based upon upon phrases and looks; in matters so minor and beside the factor that it's far unrealistic to characteristic and depend 'em up: what then? The satisfaction he offers, is as an alternative as brilliant clearly as though it value a fortune." ~ Scrooge speaking approximately Mr. Fezziwig

Fred is the nephew of Ebenezer Scrooge and the child of Scrooge's sister, Fan.

At the begin of the story, Fred welcomes his uncle over for Christmas. Scrooge desires genuinely not some thing to do with the occasion. Still, Fred safeguards Christmas:

" But I am nice I actually have constantly perception about Christmas time, while it has come spherical-- aside from the veneration because of its holy call and starting, if something coming from it is able to be apart from that-- as a remarkable time; a kind, forgiving, charitable, amusing time: the first-class time I apprehend of, inside the prolonged calendar of the 3 hundred and sixty five days, even as women and men appear through one consent to open their close to-up hearts effects, and to consider human beings right below them as although they in truth had been fellow-passengers to the tomb, and not some other race of beings certain on exceptional journeys. And because of this, uncle, even though it has by no means ever positioned a scrap of silver or gold in my pocket, I bear in mind that it has accomplished me top, and could do me applicable; and I say, God bless it!"

Ghost of Christmas Past shows Scrooge scenes from Christmas in the beyond.

" The college is not rather deserted," stated the Ghost. "A singular youngster, omitted via manner of his accurate pals, is left there despite the fact that."

Ghost of Christmas Present applications Scrooge scenes of the present Christmas.

Loaded up on the ground, to shape a form of throne, had been turkeys, ducks, hobby, hen, brawn, exquisite joints of meat, sucking-pigs, prolonged wreaths of sausages, mince-pies, plum-puddings, barrels of oysters, purple-heat chestnuts, cherry-cheeke apples, juicy oranges, luscious pears, tremendous twelfth-cakes, and seething bowls of punch, that made the chamber dim with their tasty steam. In smooth country in this sofa there sat a jolly Giant, awesome to peer, who bore a radiant torch, wholesome no longer in comparison to Plenty's horn, and held it up, immoderate up, to shed its moderate on Scrooge as he came peeping round the door.

Ghost of Christmas Yet to Come is a frightening determine who indicates Scrooge scenes from Christmas in the destiny.

" Ghost of the Future," he exclaimed, "I fear you more than any spectre I even have seen. However, as I recognise your cause is to do me suitable, and as I intend to stay to be any other guy from what I turn out to be, I'm organized to go through you enterprise, and do it with an appreciative coronary coronary coronary heart. Will you no longer talk to me?"

Jacob Marley became the business enterprise companion of Ebenezer Scrooge. He seems to Scrooge as a ghost and urges Scrooge to exchange his strategies.

" Organization!" sobbed the Ghost, wringing its hands all over again. "Humanity have become my commercial enterprise company. The normal properly-being became my commercial enterprise; charity, mercy, forbearance, and altruism, have been, all, my enterprise. The negotiations of my trade were however a drop of water within the thorough ocean of my commercial enterprise!"

Old Joe manage taken items. He appears in a scene discovered to Scrooge thru the use of the Ghost of Christmas Yet to Come.

" Open that bundle, vintage Joe, and permit me recognize the rate of it. Speak up plain. I am not scared to be the number one, nor scared for them to see it. We understood quite nicely that we had been assisting ourselves earlier than we met right here, I be given as real with. It's no sin. Open the package deal, Joe."

Ebenezer Scrooge-- No listing of A Christmas Carol Characters is probably entire without Ebenezer Scrooge. He's is the number one character of the story. We watch as he changes from a penny pincher who's best interest is cash into a man who values Christmas and its training.

Oh! But he have come to be a respectable-fisted hand on the grindstone, Scrooge! A squeezing, wrenching, know-how, scraping, clutching, covetous, antique sinner! Hard and sharp as flint, from which no metal had ever commenced out beneficiant fireplace; mystery, and self-contained, and singular as an oyster.

Dick Wilkins changed into a fellow apprentice on the equal time as Scrooge labored for Mr. Fezziwig.

Chapter 13: The Marriage Of Charles Dickens

A guy orders a bracelet for his woman friend. It is badly sent out to his domestic wherein his marriage companion well-knownshows it. Seems like a love e book does not it? Nonetheless, it honestly occurred to Charles Dickens and his companion Catherine.

Catherine Hogarth, the oldest daughter of George and Georgina Hogarth, have become born in Scotland. In 1834 she and her family transferred to England wherein her dad had taken a job as a track critic for the Early morning Chronicle.

Charles Dickens, more youthful and unattached, have emerge as moreover hired with the aid of the usage of way of the Early morning Chronicle. His first romantic courting, with Maria Beadnell, had ended badly. Nevertheless, he have emerge as as a substitute recuperated and changed into swiftly considering Catherine.

They met in 1834, ended up being participated in 1835 and were wed in April of 1836. In January of 1837 the number one in their 10 kids grow to be born.

The Happy Years

The early years of their marriage were manifestly alternatively happy. Dickens cherished his younger accomplice, and he or she changed into in fact satisfied along aspect her famous partner. In 1841 the couple headed to Scotland. In 1842 they headed to America collectively.

After the 1842 trip to America, Catherine's sister Georgina got here to live with the couple. Catherine have come to be being crushed with the responsibilities of being the associate of a famous guy and searching after their youngsters. Georgina came in to fill the regions and in the end ran the Dickens own family.

Disenchantment

Dickens grew disillusioned with Catherine and his marriage. He frowned on the fact that he had such a number of children to guide. (In a few way he saw this as Catherine's fault.) He failed to authorize of Catherine's absence of power. He started to expose that she wasn't nor had ever been his intellectual same.

In 1855 his discontent led him to just accept an invite to meet his previous sweetheart, Maria Beadnell. Maria had wed and had end up Mrs. Henry Winter season. Nevertheless Mrs. Henry Winter season did no longer degree as a brilliant deal as Dickens' romantic memories and actually no longer something ever came of the reunion.

Ellen Ternan

In 1857 Dickens met the woman who became to be his associate till his death, Ellen Ternan. Ellen, her mother and her sister had been worked with to act in a bonus talk of The Frozen Deep. The event become backed via Dickens who additionally co-starred in case.

Dickens' life with Catherine seemed loads greater unbearable after meeting Ellen. Dickens wrote to his right pal John Forster, "Poor Catherine and I aren't produced for every distinct, and there's no help for it. It is not exceptional that she makes me stressful and disenchanted, however that I make her so too-- and some distance extra so."

In 1857 Charles and Catherine took separate bedrooms.

In the spring of 1858 a bracelet that Dickens offered as a present for Ellen modified into by way of danger furnished to the Dickens own family. Catherine decided the bracelet and implicated Dickens of having an affair. Dickens denied the allegation and said it have become his custom-made to offer little provides to humans that acted in his performs.

Separation

In June of 1858 Catherine and Charles have been lawfully separated. Days later Dickens launched a notification inside the London Times and Home Words that attempted to make clear the separation to the overall public.

In the notification he stated, "Some domestic hassle of mine, of putting up with, on which I'm going to make no extra remark than that it claims to be favored, as being of a sacredly personal nature, has these days been given a plan, which includes no anger or sick-will of any type, and the whole starting, development, and surrounding conditions of that have been, all through, in the information of my children. It's agreeably made up, and its specifics have now to be forgotten by way of those worried in it."

While a assertion of this kind appears intense Dickens changed into inspired to accumulate this through a number of the evaluations dispensing about the breakup.

There have become a few chatter approximately a starlet and some tales even counseled that Dickens emerge as having an affair collectively along with his sister-in-law, Georgina. The second report changed into specially distressing due to the truth inside the ones times the form of dating could have been considered as incestuous.

Regardless of guarantees that matters were "agreeably made up" Dickens and Catherine had been by no means ever again on amusing phrases. Catherine became given a home. Their oldest little one, Charley, relocated collectively together with her. Dickens saved custody of the the rest of the youngsters. While the kids were now not prohibited to go to their mother, they have been not brought on to accomplish that.

Catherine lived for a few different a long time after the separation, in 1879. Deprived of every the area of companion and mom, she in no manner ever seemed to get well from the breakup of her marriage.

Chapter 14: The Kids Of Charles Dickens

Charles and Catherine Dickens had 10 kids. There's inconclusive evidence that Dickens and Ellen Ternan had a little one that passed away fast after being born. Nevertheless this has in no way ever been demonstrated.

Charles Culliford Boz Dickens (1837-1896) -- Charles, referred to as Charley inside the own family, changed into the oldest baby of Charles Dickens.

Charley started out his strolling existence in banking and organisation. Though, in 1868 he entered into insolvency and modified into then labored with via using using his dad to artwork at "All The All" year. Later Charley wrote the referral books, Dickens's Dictionary of London and Dickens's Dictionary of the Thames.

Charley purchased Gad's Hill Place after his dad handed away, however later gave it up clearly due to his failing fitness. He passed away in 1896 at the same time as he come to be only 59.

Mary Dickens (1838-1896) -- Mary changed into known as after her mom's sister who surpassed away in 1837. After her dad's demise she coped together with her auntie, Georgina. Mary went on to put in writing down My Daddy as I Remember Him.

Kate Macready Dickens (1839-1929) -- When Dickens and Catherine aside Kate modified into the handiest teen to face up to Dickens and side with Catherine. That must now not were a marvel to Dickens as Kate have been known as "Lucifer Box" in the own family simply due to her intense temper. She wed Charles Allston Collins and after his loss of existence she wed Carlo Perugini.

Walter Landor Dickens (1841-1863) -- Walter modified into known as after the writer and poet, Walter Savage Landor.

Walter performed the rank of lieutenant inside the East India Company. It regarded loads like he had a terrific future, however regretfully topics began to break down for Walter. Like an entire lot of his contributors of the family he fell right into cash debt. At about this time he also ended up being unwell. He died of an aortic aneurysm and left many overdue charges to his dad.

Francis Jeffrey Dickens (1844-1886) -- Francis became nicknamed "Chickenstalker" by way of the usage of his dad. The name is from a person in The Chimes.

Francis considered many professions consisting of drugs, farming and journalism. He wound up signing up with the Bengal Mounted Cops. Later he signed up with Canada's Northwest Mounted Authorities. In 1886 he resigned his fee and died inside the three hundred and sixty five days.

Alfred D'Orsay Tennyson Dickens (1845-1912) -- When he changed into twenty

Alfred left England, and additionally many unsettled fees, and went to Australia. There he wed the "Belle of Melbourne", Jessie Devlin. Unfortunately she exceeded away in a carriage mishap 4 years later leaving Alfred by myself with their 2 girls.

After his dad's loss of life Alfred gave lectures on his dad's lifestyles and paintings.

Sydney Smith Haldimand Dickens (1847-1872) -- Charles Dickens become distinctly pleased with Sydney's marine career. Nevertheless, later he was pretty displeased about Sydney's economic issues. Sydney died on the same time as he changed into fine twenty five. He exceeded away while seeking to cross returned domestic for prison leave.

Henry Fielding Dickens (1849-1933) -- Henry modified into nicknamed Harry and is typically known as the only of Dickens' youngsters. He have turn out to be a sportsperson and had a certainly powerful profession in regulation. In 1922 he became knighted.

Henry changed into the grandpa of Monica Dickens who ended up being a author like her great grandpa. Amongst her works is One Set of Hands.

Dora Annie Dickens (1850-1851) -- Dora have turn out to be known as after a person from in truth one in every of her dad's books, Dora from David Copperfield. Dora changed into by no means ever a sturdy toddler and handed away even as she changed into best eight months vintage.

Edward Bulwer Lytton Dickens (1852-1902) -- Edward have become nicknamed Plorn. He became known as after the author Edward Bulwer-Lytton. As an fascinating aside, the quote "it become a darkish and moist night" originates from Bulwer-Lytton's e-book Paul Clifford.

Edward left England to sign up for his brother Alfred in Australia. Sometime after that, he ended up being a Member of Parliament in New South Wales.

Chapter 15: Master Of His Own Future

"It come to be the first rate of times, it end up the worst of instances, it became the age of consciousness, it have become the age of foolishness, it emerge as the epoch of belief, it have become the epoch of incredulity, it become the season of moderate, it end up the season of darkness, it modified into the spring of want, it became the wintry climate of melancholy, we had the entirety in advance than us, we had nothing before us, we had been all going direct to Heaven, we had been all going direct the possibility manner – in quick, the duration become to this point similar to the prevailing length, that some of its noisiest government insisted on its being obtained, for suited or for evil, inside the superlative degree of assessment handiest."

Although it could be complicated to place the ones strains exactly, they will be certainly very acquainted, and their author, the exquisite author Charles Dickens is even greater widely recognized than the prolific phrases that have been his legacy to past, gift and future generations. Many writers have taken on the position of social commentator down via the a long time, but few were answerable for instigating the degree of social trade Charles Dickens controlled to collect. From the plight of the workhouse born Oliver Twist to the impecunious Mr Micawber, Dickens furnished his readers with a glimpse into the darker element of Victorian life, which ran parallel with the technology's sentimentality, and the superb and the great of the age had been pressured to remember the plight of the terrible.

But first and predominant, Charles Dickens emerge as a tremendous storyteller, possibly one of the very high-quality the arena has ever recognized, and extra charming although than his repertoire of novels and his large stable of colorful characters is the author's personal lifestyles, proving past all low-value doubt that fact is, constantly, stranger than fiction.

So, as we start our adventure again in time to enter the charming global of Charles Dickens, the relevance of our starting strains turns into ever extra poignant, reflecting the writer's all-seeing eye and his precise portrayal of the human situation. And whether you'd need to have a take a look at on or need to apprehend which novel the ones acquainted words open, at the following pub quiz, the solution is "A Tale of Two Cities", Charles Dickens' shifting account of the horrors and heroes of the French Revolution.

However, OUR story of Charles Dickens starts offevolved far, an prolonged manner from the dramatically dashing and romantic streets of Paris and the primary port of name has to the very aptly named Portsmouth on England's south coast. Here, in very modest surroundings Charles John Huffam Dickens got here into the arena on the 7th of February 1812, a Friday, and whether or no longer the activities had been without a doubt as he defined at the same time as he opened his maximum automobile-biographical novel, David Copperfield" we're able to only danger a well-informed guess.

"To begin my lifestyles with the start of my lifestyles, I file that I even have emerge as born (as I have been knowledgeable and accept as true with) on a Friday, at twelve o'clock at night time time time. It have emerge as remarked that the clock started to strike, and I started to cry, concurrently."

Portsmouth, to in recent times remains a Naval metropolis, and the highlight for many traffic who come proper proper right here is HMS Victory, the sector-famous flagship of Admiral Lord Nelson. It turn out to be aboard this deliver that Nelson turn out to be killed at the Battle of Trafalgar in 1805 on the pinnacle of his exceptional victory over the French Fleet. Britain have been at warfare with France for the reason that 1803, as Napoleon Bonaparte had stormed to power within the aftermath of the French Revolution, and irrespective of the fact that Nelson have emerge as a fulfillment on the Battle of Trafalgar, the warfare endured until 1815, while Napoleon modified into ultimately defeated on the Battle of Waterloo.

For the number one few years of Charles Dickens' lifestyles the Navy have turn out to be on immoderate alert at Portsmouth, and more youthful Charles's father, John, changed into gainfully employed at the Naval Pay Office. But because the Napoleonic Wars had been drawing to a near, the Navy come to be able to lessen its presence in Portsmouth and John Dickens, along collectively with his circle of relatives in tow, have come to be called again to paintings at Somerset House in London. This supposed a widespread drop in income, and far from prospering, John Dickens modified into accruing excessive debt.

By the time the Dickens family moved to Chatham in 1816, wherein there has been a busy Naval Dockyard, John Dickens changed into however dwelling past the technique of a Pay Office Clerk.

For devotees of Charles Dickens, a go to to 11 Ordnance Terrace is truely at the pilgrim's path, notwithstanding the fact that whilst he lived here it become truely variety 2, and of path the Railway Station, now contrary, did now not exist. Charles and his older sister Fanny, fortunately accomplished in the hay place that then stretched out inside the the the front of the house, and have been blissfully blind to the issues in advance, all through the ones very satisfied days.

In reality a number of Charles Dickens maximum evocative writing stemmed from happy memories of early children, and few humans apprehend that Dickens is certainly responsible for our pre-profession with there being snow at Christmas. For the primary 8 years of Charles Dickens' lifestyles, it snowed each Christmas, and when he wrote about the festive time of 3 hundred and sixty five days in later existence, he commonly ensured a blanket of snow included the placing of each scene.

Even within the 19th Century this changed into pretty a run of White Christmases, and inside the whole 20th Century there have been quality valid White Christmases, in 1938 and 1970. As a writer, Charles Dickens remembered the ones happier instances, whilst snow simply befell to seem at Christmas, and although it would be many years later, the have an impact on this will have on the Great British notion of Christmas, via Dickens' festive services, have become now not some component short of extra special.

And it wasn't most effective the climate which have grow to be lodged in Charles Dickens' subconscious, because of the fact the folks who he got here into contact with would possibly moreover be stored up for destiny reference. Without doubt, his nursemaid, Mary Weller, who thrilled her more youthful fee with gory recollections of gothic horror, stimulated the boy's growing creativeness at the same time as the Dickens circle of relatives lived at Ordnance Terrace, and she or he later made an appearance in David Copperfield because the more youthful hero's nursemaid, Peggotty.

Nevertheless, just like any of Charles Dickens' brilliant novels, trouble have become in no way a ways away, and grow to be simply already brewing due to John Dickens' growing indebtedness. As the circle of relatives grew in duration topics worsened, and they moved from Ordnance Terrace to inexpensive resorts in Chatham, which for a brief whilst supplied a bit stability, and Charles even attended school for a fast spell.

Chatham has in no way been appeared due to the fact the maximum picturesque of the Medway towns, so named due to their closeness to the River Medway, however neighbouring Rochester has certainly earned recognition of its attraction and has grow to be a completely famous traveler enchantment. With an imposing Norman Castle, terrific Cathedral and cobbled streets, Rochester could have been created thru Charles Dickens as a backdrop for any of his novels, but it became of path, quite the alternative manner round. During his years at Chatham as a more youthful boy, Charles had been given to recognise Rochester properly, and some of the places, which in spite of the truth that stand to at the existing time, can in fact be recognized inside the memories that he informed.

From the Royal Victoria and Bull Hotel, in which the Adventures of Mr Samuel Pickwick started out, to the incredible Restoration House that end up the version for Miss Haversham's cobwebbed mansion in Great Expectations, you can discover evidence of Dickens passing this manner, quite tons everywhere. And the person himself has come to be a fantastic a part of Rochester's Tourist Industry, bringing loads of literary visitors to the southeast. With a Dickensian Summer and Christmas Festival held every 365 days, and reminders of Dickens and his most famous novels anywhere you appearance, we're able to see virtually how large recollections from adolescence might display to be at the same time as Dickens commenced out his writing profession.

Chapter 16: Dark Days For Charles Dickens

Despite John Dickens' inability to control the own family budget, there has been a near bond among father and son. The pair must take long walks via the Medway cities and the encompassing geographical area, taking element in every others employer, and they regularly surpassed a pleasant assets on Higham Hill, overlooking Rochester that have been built in 1780 for the Lord Mayor.

Gad's Hill Place absolutely appealed to the little boy, and John Dickens informed his son that if he worked in fact difficult in life, he could possibly in the future come to live in it. Whether he in reality believed this or have become in reality telling an extraordinary tale to inspire his son, we'll in no manner recognize, however as we'll discover most effective a bit later, this could show to be one of the few topics that John Dickens virtually were given right!

Nevertheless, as time moved on, even the delight of a rustic stroll became to be denied young Charles as in 1822 the own family moved once more, to London's Camden Town, wherein John Dickens' financial problems got here to a head. Charles come to be honestly twelve years old while his mom took steps to enhance the own family price range with the beneficial aid of arranging with a relative for the boy to begin art work in his boot blacking manufacturing facility.

That the revel in changed into the most humiliating viable for the touchy Charles who had completed nicely at faculty is undoubted, and the way it made him enjoy has been recorded for posterity in the novel David Copperfield, and to three degree Oliver Twist, however internal days things went from awful to worse.

Without manner, lifestyles in Victorian London become very difficult, and for John Dickens, without a friend or relation left to whom he did now not owe coins, the Debtor's Prison loomed large. As Charles started out out paintings at the blacking manufacturing facility, John Dickens end up arrested and thrown into the infamous Marshalsea, and his spouse and own family, besides for Charles, who have turn out to be in inns, went with him.

These had been dark days for Charles Dickens, and exhausted from labouring in the boot blacking manufacturing facility, he felt on my own and abandoned. Already the precious reminiscences of Chatham and Rochester would possibly have been essential in helping him thru hard days and lonely nights, even as any thoughts of what the destiny could possibly deliver have been very bleak actually.

What occurred next come to be as remarkably lucky as some thing you may concentrate in a Fairy Story, as an inheritance came John Dickens' manner pretty . Restored to respectability, he another time to his former function as a Naval Pay Roll Clerk at Somerset House, and right now removed Charles from the blacking production facility, determined the boy have to maintain his studies.

It will in all likelihood come as a few thing of a wonder that Mrs Dickens disagreed entire heartedly together with her husband's actions, and she or he insisted young Charles be despatched decrease again to the blacking manufacturing facility, but Mr Dickens grow to be adamant, and Charles end up despatched to Wellington House Academy.

It didn't take lengthy but for John Dickens to slip once more into his vintage strategies, and after years Charles' training must not be paid for. Even so he modified into now nicely geared up to make his way within the global, and his mother decided him a miles higher function than the previous way in the manufacturing unit, and he have come to be a junior clerk with the prison professionals, Ellis and Blakemore.

At very last Charles Dickens grow to be draw close of his private future and he quick started out out to prosper, progressing to grow to be a Parliamentary Reporter on the House of Commons.

After falling in love and being deemed unsuitable via using the woman in question's circle of relatives because of his non-public doubtful records, it is believed Charles became to writing for consolation. By threat he had inadvertently determined a herbal capabilities, and by using the use of 1834 comedian reminiscences, courtesy of his pen call "Boz", started out to seem in the magazines of the day. In turn this brought about a function as a reporter at the Morning Chronicle, and it need to have been a excellent consolation whilst the younger Mr Charles Dickens esquire changed into capable to interrupt loose from his family and take rooms for himself at Furnival's Inn, Holborn.

And so, the writing career of Charles Dickens had all started, due to the reality the number one of his novels, "The Pickwick Papers", made its debut in 1836. It is beneficial proper right here to do not forget how novels have been usually published right now, because it does glide an prolonged way to explaining why the young creator rapid have end up a publishing phenomenon. The Pickwick Papers, which observed the adventures of the eponymous hero and the no longer going humans of a carrying club, as they travelled across the geographical place, have become posted in twenty monthly instalments.

www.ingramcontent.com/pod-product-compliance
Lightning Source LLC
Chambersburg PA
CBHW071440080526
44587CB00014B/1927